RELIGION AND
THE EUROPEAN MIND

THE STONE LECTURES

DELIVERED AT PRINCETON UNIVERSITY

(*Under the title "Religion and Revolution"*)

REVISED AND ENLARGED
WITH ADDITIONAL NOTES AND APPEN-
DICES GIVING THE FULL TEXT OF THE
CONSTITUTIONAL DOCUMENTS CITED

IT is impossible to understand the German Church Revolution without a knowledge of the theological background. This controversy is here set forth as a prelude to a statement of the fundamental spiritual problem with which all Evangelical Churches will be confronted sooner or later.

The Appendices include the Constitution of the German Evangelical Church, the Concordat between the Vatican and the German Government, the resolutions of the Free National Synod at Barmen, May 31, 1934, and other important documents.

★

"No one desiring to understand and penetrate the significance of contemporary Christianity can afford to neglect this volume and its philosophical interpretation of current Christian history."

CHARLES S. MACFARLAND,

General Secretary Emeritus of the Federal Council of the Churches of Christ in America.

RELIGION AND THE
EUROPEAN MIND

The L. P. Stone Lectures, Princeton Theological Seminary, 1933

RELIGION
AND
THE EUROPEAN MIND

By

ADOLF KELLER, D.D., LL.D.
(Universities of Zürich and Geneva)
The International Christian Social Institute, Geneva

LONDON
THE LUTTERWORTH PRESS
4 BOUVERIE STREET, E.C. 4

First published in 1934
(in U.S.A. as "Religion and Revolution")

BOOKS BY DR. ADOLF KELLER

RELIGION AND THE EUROPEAN MIND

DYNAMIS: A CONSIDERATION OF THE FORMS AND
FORCES OF AMERICAN PROTESTANTISM

PROTESTANT EUROPE (with George Stewart)

KARL BARTH AND CHRISTIAN UNITY

[*Made in Great Britain*]

CONTENTS

AUTHOR'S FOREWORD

In publishing these Stone Lectures, which were delivered at The Theological Seminary in Princeton, New Jersey, in November 1933, I wish first of all to thank the faculty of that seminary for the opportunity they gave me once more to interpret the religious life of one continent to the people of another. Such interpretations have now been my special task for more than a decade. In a first volume, entitled *Dynamis: A Consideration of the Forms and Forces of American Protestantism*, I tried to give a picture of American Church life to our Continental Churches. In a second volume, *Protestant Europe*, published jointly with my friend, George Stewart, we tried to present a picture of European Church life to the English-speaking world. A book on *Karl Barth and Christian Unity* dealt with the main theological currents in the various Churches and with their relation to contemporaneous and ecclesiastical movements. These Lectures are a direct sequel to this last book in so far as they analyse the religious conflict with which this movement is now so closely involved.

This volume does not deal primarily with Church history or with the rapidly changing aspects of European Church life, but with the deeper fundamental problems which underlie the present changes in the religious life of Europe. It describes

6

the last and final decision with which Continental theology is confronted in the midst of a revolution which is overthrowing old political systems and the moral philosophy of a generation. Recent events have made it sufficiently clear that a religious battle cannot be fought on the surface of a daily changing party conflict, but only in that depth of Church thinking where the question of truth is the sole and fundamental concern.

In presenting these Lectures to an American public,[1] I became aware that the present theological conflicts are not confined to the European Continent. They are to be found in America as well as in Europe, wherever the political and social conflicts, the restlessness of the human soul, the chaotic conditions of human relations, the uncertainty of the Christian conscience, point to a deeper and invisible revolution in the religious mind of our generation.

A reorientation is needed and is being sought. This is, perhaps, the basic meaning of the present revolutionary movements. A great effort is being made to ascertain whether the Reformation, through its rediscovery of the Gospel, has not again a message for our time.

I have to thank my friends, Dr. Douglas Horton and Dr. Wilhelm Pauck, for the revision of these lectures and for help in preparing them for publi-

[1] It should be clearly understood that these Lectures deal primarily with the fundamental principles which underlie the revolutionary events in Europe. It is not yet possible to write a detailed history of the events that are now taking place. The scenes of the drama change almost daily, but the theme remains the same.

7

cation. I am especially indebted to Professor Pauck who, after my return to Switzerland, corrected the manuscript on the basis of additional material which I sent him, and who has contributed certain significant formulations which clarify the meaning of the constantly changing events.

In preparing this edition for England I have made several important additions, bringing the information up to date in every particular; and the official documents contained in the six appendices will be valuable to many readers for constant reference purposes. I am indebted to Dr. Macfarland for the English text of the Constitution (Appendix I) and of the National Concordat (Appendix V).

A. K.

GENEVA
June 7, 1934

I

INTRODUCTION

RELIGION AND REVOLUTION

THESE Lectures on Contemporary Christianity on the European Continent deal, for the most part, with the deeper aspects of religious life which have come to light during the various revolutions in Europe. Revolution and religion are to-day far more closely related than they were during the French Revolution, when Christianity was replaced by the "Cult of Reason," and when Napoleon had no use for the "hypothesis of an Almighty God."

The revolutions of the twentieth century have emerged, consciously or unconsciously, from a religious background; they can hardly escape being considered religious problems. They could not have captured the imagination of the masses and demanded their tremendous sacrifices if there were not in them an underlying mysticism of a religious character. The leading ideas of the French Revolution, *Liberté, Egalité, Fraternité*, have a philosophical connotation. These concepts have to-day lost their magic spell. The *idées-forces* of the present revolutions have a religious, not a philosophical, character. This is true of the Bolshevist quite as much as of the nationalistic revolutions. They are not mere political movements nor do they aim merely at the transformation of the social structure of mankind.

9

They are not a battle for privileges for a certain class or group, but the result of a new vision of humanity as a whole, the expression of a new mystical faith in man and his creative faculties. They have developed creeds for which millions are willing to suffer and to die. They have their Messiahs, apostles and martyrs who inspire the masses with a feeling of adoration and with the hope of salvation and victory. They have adopted symbols which have exercised a profound influence upon the collective imagination, and they are teaching an eschatology which anticipates a day of Judgment and a Kingdom to come. Bolshevism and Nationalism are new national religions hidden in political and social programmes.

Christianity is here confronted again with that natural religious force immanent in the human soul which is capable of glorifying and transfiguring new desires, life instincts and ideals, and which grows luxuriantly in the hotbed of revolution. A religious halo surrounds the new symbols. The leaders exercise a veritable fascination on millions who no longer understand the simple message of Jesus Christ, but are ready to believe in a political or social mysticism. Once again Christianity must struggle with "principalities and powers," with mysterious and demonic forces, clad in all the glamour of a new hope and a new vision.

They are all the more dangerous to Christianity because they are penetrating the public life of states and nations, and even the Christian Church as such. They constitute, therefore, aggressive powers from without and dangerous, invisible influences from within.

Where the revolution has assumed an avowedly hostile attitude towards the Christian Church, as in *Russia*, Christians know that, as in the first centuries, they must again learn the lesson of martyrdom and the Cross. The Church must again descend into the catacombs, because the "beast from the abyss" is rising to rule the earth. The Christian faith is tolerated by law, but is oppressed by an all-powerful party which is purging the country of religion, the "opiate for the people." Christian evangelism is replaced by atheistic propaganda. Religious education for young people under eighteen years of age is prohibited, while godless education is assisted with the powerful propaganda of the Press, the films, and all the resources of a blasphemous art. Ministers of the Christian religion are refused the privileges of the working class—the bread-card, for instance—and hundreds, even thousands, have been condemned to starvation and death. In punishment for confessing a religion other than that of the State, twenty-four of the seventy Lutheran pastors still living in Russia are in concentration camps—some in the northern forests, others in the remote vastnesses of Siberia.

Innumerable churches have been closed or transformed into motion-picture theatres or museums. Upon others such burdensome taxes have been levied that the congregations can no longer hold them. It would be idle to discuss whether these actions constitute religious persecution or simply political oppression. It cannot be denied, at any rate, that the religious policy of the Soviets is hostile to the Christian religion—if not in its ordinances. at least in its practices; most of all in the attitude of the Third International.

We might try to interpret this hostility as a reaction against the former Russian Orthodox Church, which was so closely identified with the Tsarist régime and the capitalistic structure of the old society. The revolution might then be understood as Nemesis overtaking a Church which was mystical, ritualistic and hierarchic; oblivious to the misery and suffering of the people, neglectful of the social problem as no other Christian Church has ever been.

A deeper insight into the spirit of the Soviet policy, and especially into the tendencies of the "godless movement," reveals, however, that we are confronted not merely with a reaction against an unsocial Christianity, but with a new conception of life, hostile in principle to Christianity and Christian ideals, since it is in itself a new religion, competing with the old one in every field. It is a religion of science, believing in the almighty power of reason and its redemptive faculties. Salvation is seen in the collective social effort of mankind. It is the religion of humanism or secularism based on faith in the mystical, redemptive and constructive capacity of man. It is a religion of idealism in so far as an idea or vision of man is the starting-point for a huge constructive effort on behalf of society.

A large part of the American public, especially the young people, are so much interested in this constructive social effort, this new and hopeful social experiment, that no attention is paid to the underlying mystical forces in the Russian Revolution and to its invisible attack on the religious and moral values of our Christian era. Europe, being nearer to the spiritual sources of the Russian Revolution, and feeling its influence in every field of public life, is much more aware of this religious aspect of Russian Communism. Christians in Russia, Orthodox as well as Protestant, speak openly of the new era of Antichrist, while the Churches of the Continent must struggle against this anti-Christian propaganda not only among the labouring classes but in the parliaments—and even in the universities. If the German Church has so readily accepted the National Socialist revolution, this acceptance, to a large extent, is due to the fact that the political revolution saved it from a religious revolution inspired by Bolshevist ideals and stimulated by the communist anti-Christian upheaval.

How one such anti-Christian communist movement dealt with the Church may be seen in Hungary, and again in Spain, where burning monasteries and churches became a *fanal* for an attack on the dominating Roman Church. Nevertheless, the religious problem connected with the *Spanish Revolution* is more complicated than this open hostility would seem to indicate. Communism, as such, is in principle set against organized religion,

13

since the latter has been a virtual ally of the old capitalistic and bourgeois society. But Spanish communists with whom the writer has spoken declare that they are fighting only against the clericalism and Jesuitism of the Roman Catholic Church, against a Church of power and wealth and political influence—not against the Church as such, the social activity of which they appreciate. The Spanish people are evidently so deeply impregnated with the religious spirit of the Catholic Church that they can never be wholly obsessed by the anti-Christian hatred which actuates the Russian Bolshevists.

This influence of tradition in Spain also explains the religious attitude of the intellectual *élite* who came into power with the revolution. They had to discover and establish a spiritual and metaphysical foundation for the State, and their political example was France. But French positivism and scepticism could not provide the Spanish people with an adequate philosophy for a new social and political structure. Philosophers like Don Giner de los Rios and Fernando de los Rios (the latter has been Minister of Education) discovered in Erasmus a religious force which was Catholic and modern at the same time, deeply concerned with the mystical fellowship of the Church, and yet open to the reformation of the whole collective life. Don Luís de Zulueta, formerly Minister of Foreign Affairs, and now ambassador at Berlin, may be considered as a typical example of the modern Spaniard— deeply religious and even Catholic, and yet anti-

14

clerical and anti-Jesuitical. In a book, *La Oración del Incrédulo*, this anti-clerical and anti-Jesuit "unbeliever" expresses a mystical love of Christ as well as the deep yearning of an earnest Christian heart for a Church of religious inspiration and of moral and social influence. For him the revolution does not mean the destruction of the Christian ideal, but a new possibility of realizing it, an opportunity to liberate the Christian Church from the cloak of its pride, its love for wealth and political influence, and to lead it back to its high spiritual, educational and social task.

The first President of the Council, Azaña, would hardly have translated Borrow's *The Bible in Spain* into Spanish were he not a believer in the constructive and uplifting forces of the Gospel. The philosopher of the Spanish revolution, Unamuno, teaches a tragic pessimism in his *El Sentimiento Trágico de la Vida*, a book of a deeply religious character and evidently influenced by the Christian ideas of the Danish philosopher, Kierkegaard. The religious thinkers of the Spanish revolution seem, therefore, to be aware of the danger in the "this worldliness" of the communist religion, and to be confronting it with the "other worldliness" of a tragic eschatological pessimism which is inherent in the original Christian faith.

At any rate, Protestantism owes to the Spanish Revolution the grant of religious liberty. Hitherto the Protestant Church had been scarcely tolerated in Spain. The law did not permit the building of Protestant churches along the main streets; it prohibited inscriptions on church walls which might indicate the religious character of the building; it forbade the erection of steeples. Protestantism had to remain hidden in back streets. When King Gustav of Sweden, on the occasion of a visit to Spain some years ago, received an expression of thanks from a high dignitary of the Roman Catholic Church for the freedom which Catholics enjoyed in Sweden, he answered that he wished he could say the same for the Protestants in Spain! Revolution to-day means religious liberty to these small groups of Protestants who have maintained their faith through centuries of oppression.

The Fascist Revolution in *Italy* likewise has granted religious liberty, and thereby realized the ideal of the great Italian statesman, Cavour, who had always propagated the idea of a *chiesa libera in stato libero* (a free Church in a free State).

The Protestant Churches are no longer merely *tolerated*, they enjoy full legal protection. During the negotiations between the State and the Vatican their religious liberty was threatened up to the last moment. The Curia had expressed the desire that in recognition of the sacred history of the Eternal City as the seat of the Holy Father and the goal of Catholic pilgrimage, everything should be avoided which could alter the Catholic character of the city. But the Fascist Revolution stood firmly for the principle of religious liberty and did not approve a proposition which could easily have become a dangerous instrument of oppression in the hands of a powerful State Church. The Fascist Revolution also settled the old dispute between the Vatican and the Italian State. According to the terms of the historic Concordat, which put an end to the conflict between the Pope and the Italian Government, Church and State now mutually recognize each other in their respective spheres. Mussolini accepted in principle the spiritual and temporal power of the Pope, but did not surrender one iota of the rights of the State, and objected vigorously to the interference of the Church in the field of education.

While in the Fascist Revolution the religious question appeared more as an ecclesiastical problem—that is, as the old dispute between Church and State, the German Revolution has brought to light problems of a deeply and authentically religious nature. The national revolution there is paralleled by a religious revolution. Not only does it aim at the unification of the various Churches on a national basis, but it has called forth a religion of modern paganism, which has entered the lists against the old Christian confessions.

At the present time a tremendous religious battle is raging in the soul of *Germany*. We might call it *the struggle of secular religion against the Christian Gospel*. It began with a fight for power in the field of Church politics. While this fight has by no means ended, it has become clear to the leaders that in a spiritual struggle, such as this is, a decision cannot be reached by the application of force, but only by a sincere search for truth, and a willingness to apply it. The struggle, therefore, is concentrated in a mighty theological controversy. It is a unique spectacle to see the political and ecclesiastical promoters of a revolution involving themselves in theological subtleties and ultimate religious principles. They have had to do so. Doctrines of creation and revelation have become slogans in the battle for an adequate religion. They have had to be affirmed or refuted. Luther has become the spokesman for a new conception of State and Nation. The German Revolution has awakened not only the political instincts and deep metaphysical dreams of a great nation, but also the religious passions which were thought to have been buried long ago. It is a revolution with a theology.

Present-day Germany presents, therefore, a most illuminating example of a battle of universals, a struggle between fundamental conceptions of religious values, between religion as a natural element of higher human life on the one hand, and as revealed Christian faith on the other; a battle in which the Christian Churches of all lands must be immensely interested. This battle between natural religion and the Gospel is being fought everywhere, in one form or another. It cannot be decided by powerful parties, by governmental decrees, by ecclesiastical compromises. The solution can only be found where Christian theology is patient enough to ask the eternal question: *"What is Truth?"* What does the Bible really say? What does Jesus Christ mean for us?

The chapters which follow indicate how, in the midst of the turmoil of a revolution, these questions are again emerging—and demanding a clear, direct answer. He who has ears to hear will be aware that in our description of a particular situation we are speaking of a general revolution in Christian thinking for which the German situation is only a paradigm.

A problem of such magnitude cannot be solved at the periphery of political considerations, or by educational or social efforts, but only at the centre of the life of the Church, where she is confronted with the inescapable question as to what is the truth for which she is willing to live—or to die.

The German example is illuminating from still another point of view. It is an undeniable fact that the mother country of the Reformation has also been, to a large extent, the birthplace of new theological problems. Most of the new theological theories and schools of the last century originated in Germany and Switzerland: the theology of a rational *a priori* as well as the theology of the religious consciousness or of Christian experience; the Ritschlian school as well as that of comparative religion; Biblical criticism as well as religious socialism and Barthianism. The theological labours of other countries have not been so much directed to universal theological problems; they have made specific contributions to special fields: textual criticism and patristic studies have long prevailed in Great Britain; confessional theology in Sweden and Holland; religious psychology and education in

America. This, of course, must be taken *cum grano salis*, since theological interests migrate from one country to another.

Continental theology of recent years has, for the most part, been stimulated by and occupied with problems originating in Germany and Switzerland. This whole Continental theological network, of the Lutheran as well as of the Reformed type, is being put to the test by the present German Revolution. In this revolution a new form of *theologia naturalis*, a secular or humanistic religion, has come to the front, and a controversy of the first magnitude between it and the revealed religion of the Christian Gospel has resulted. The German situation is only one example of this ultimate dispute between the two forms of religion. In the following chapters, therefore, we shall not concern ourselves with the daily changing aspects and events of the present struggle between State and Church and between the parties within the Church, but shall confine ourselves to those fundamental problems which will persist until a solution has been found by earnest theological rethinking of the old positions.

These problems have been ripening during the last fifteen years. They were present everywhere in the religious situation. The revolution has brought them out into open conflict, into a struggle which, even if a truce be granted, cannot come to an end for many a year.

Protestantism all over the world is participating in the struggle, because it is everywhere felt: *tua res agitur*. Our own religious life is involved, the battle is on between the truth that comes from God and the truths that come from man. Four centuries ago the Reformation fought the same battle.

We will, therefore, begin the next chapter with a reconsideration of what the Reformation meant, how its meaning was lost and how it was rediscovered, how therefore the weapons were prepared and sharpened for the present-day battle for evangelical truth and religious liberty.

II

THE REBIRTH OF THE SPIRIT OF THE REFORMATION

I. THE FUNDAMENTAL PRINCIPLE OF THE REFORMATION

THE great discovery of the reformers, the basic principle of the Reformation, was "justification by faith." The reformers did not find this principle in ecclesiastical tradition or in their religious experience, but in the New Testament, especially in the Gospel and the Pauline Epistles. Against all ecclesiastical tradition they maintained that the Bible must be considered the final and authoritative source in all matters of faith. The Bible has, therefore, been called the formal principle of the Reformation. But the *articulus stantis et cadentis ecclesiae* is the belief that man is saved by God's grace and by God's grace alone. In the *sola gratia, sola fide*, we hear the beating heart of the Reformation.

All the reformers, Luther as well as Zwingli and Calvin, are in full agreement in their belief in the sovereignty of God's grace. In this respect there is no difference between the *sola gratia* of Luther and the *soli Deo gloria* of Calvin.

The Reformation expressed its protest against all attempts of man to save himself, to find by himself the way towards God, to accomplish God's will by his own moral or religious efforts, or to attribute any meritorious effect to his own attempt to please God. This protest, therefore, excludes that Pelagianism or synergism which in the history of Christianity has always been the great temptation of the pious man, and which was a potent instrument for the Reformation in its long struggle with Roman Catholicism. The Roman doctrine of the *analogia entis*, the analogy between the Divine and human existence, or of the *imago Dei*, teaches that man can collaborate with God and work out his own salvation by meritorious works and obedience to the laws and rules of the Church.

All the Protestant Churches on the Continent are built on the basis of this fundamental principle of the Reformation. The Lutheran Church lays stress on the formula *sola fide*, while the Reformed Church emphasizes the formula *soli Deo gloria*, but these formulae represent only two aspects of the same doctrine of God's sovereign grace. The same principle is contained in the Thirty-nine Articles of the Anglican Church.

Justification by faith is so entirely the centre of the original Protestant doctrine that even Protestant ethics and practical activity have been focussed on it. In Protestant ethics sanctification is regarded not as a complementary human effort which crowns the Divine work of salvation, but rather as the result of the acceptance of God's forgiveness by the sinner, of his justification by the forensic act and judgment of God. Against all other authority—

23

the authority of the Church, the Pope, tradition, or the human *ratio*—the Reformation established as sole authority the Word of God, with its essential announcement of God's free pardon to the sinner and its claim upon the whole life of man.

2. THE EXTENSION OF THE REFORMATION

This message of the Reformation has conquered a large part of the Continent. From the cradle of the Reformation in Germany and Switzerland the movement has spread over the neighbouring countries. Lutheranism expanded mostly among the Germanic peoples in the northern and Baltic countries; even in Russia there are still about seventy Lutheran pastors who, despite persecution and suffering, are maintaining the great spiritual message of the Reformation in that atheistic country. Lutheranism extends also into Roumania where the Saxon tribes, who over seven hundred years ago migrated and settled in Transylvania, have kept their German language and maintained their evangelical faith ever since the time of the Reformation. In Poland, Hungary, Jugo-Slavia, and Czechoslovakia, there are large Lutheran minorities, all bound to the Mother Church of the Reformation through Luther's *sola fide*.

From Zürich and Geneva, the towns of Zwingli and Calvin, the Reformed movement spread over Switzerland, France, Holland, Hungary and Scotland, and, later, to America. There was a time when even Anglican bishops listened to what was said in Geneva and Zürich.

Belief in the *sola fide* and the *soli Deo gloria* has indeed conquered a whole world. It is without doubt the deepest spiritual bond between the American and European Churches, Lutheran as well as Reformed and Presbyterian.

This message inaugurated a new culture for humanity. It was elaborated in the sixteenth and seventeenth centuries in certain great symbols, such as the Confession of Augsburg, the four-hundredth anniversary of which was celebrated in 1930. In spite of the fact that the Augsburg Confession does not recognize the Reformed movement, the Reformed Churches sent their delegates to the celebration, showing thereby that they were able to forget minor differences for the sake of the common faith in the *sola fide*. The most important Reformed instruments are the *Confessio Helvetica posterior*, the Heidelberg Catechism, and the Canons of the Synod of Dort. Together with the Augsburg Confession, they are still recognized confessions of faith for large Lutheran and Reformed bodies on the Continent, a sacred heritage, an unextinguished light which begins to shine again in the darkness of our time.

3. THE HARMONIZING OF THE PRINCIPLE OF THE REFORMATION WITH THE PRINCIPLE OF MODERN CULTURE

How was it possible that a central article of faith could be diluted, misunderstood and partly forgotten for more than a century among many Continental Protestants?

25

The Gospel is the transcendental, supernatural message, coming as a light into a world which does not understand it. It is the main task of the Christian Church to announce this Gospel to a world which in its autonomy is opposed to a message establishing another authority than that of the world itself and of its laws. Christian apologetics and theology in general have, therefore, always considered it to be their task to interpret the Gospel to this hostile world, to build a bridge between Christ and this world, to interpret this message in terms of the world and to assimilate the Divine truth with the truth which the world has already discovered. Since the Renaissance and the rise of the humanistic and Cartesian philosophies this modern world has desired autonomy. The Renaissance discovered the independent and autonomous individual. Descartes established the principle, *cogito ergo sum*, which deduces existence from the free act of man's thinking. The modern world became thereby egocentric. These first sparks of a new humanistic and rationalistic autonomy of thought and moral action spread like wildfire in the respective periods of the French Encyclopaedists, of the Enlightenment and of German Idealism. The common denominator underlying these various philosophies was faith in man, in the general law of reason, in man's capacity to understand and to rule the world with the law of his intellect. In the French Revolution, when Robespierre erected an altar to the Goddess of Reason, there was exemplified the general attitude which identified the natural intellectual capacity of man with reason and with the Divine Principle itself. In the philosophy of Kant human conscience and its immanent law was identified with the cosmic law. The result was the commandment, "Thou canst, because thou oughtest." In the philosophy of Fichte the constructive will of man became the supreme principle of the State; and in the philosophy of Hegel the rhythm of the universe was interpreted as the natural rhythm of human logic. As a result of associating the constructive will of man with the rhythm of the universe, the State became an ideal entity of such perfection that it could be compared with the Kingdom of God.

Christian theology has deferred to this attitude. Schleiermacher inaugurated a modern theology which no longer took as its point of departure the Divine message, but based itself on a certain quality of the religious consciousness. Christian piety became the essence of Christianity. The Divine act of revelation was no longer the exclusive subject of theology. The general notion of "religion" became a second principle in the moral and religious philosophy of the "Enlightenment." For Kant, for instance, it was quite natural to establish such an autonomous human principle and to put it in juxtaposition to revelation. The subject of his religious philosophy was, so to speak, revelation *and* reason; but the point of departure in his book, *Religion Within the Limits of Reason*, was not revelation, but reason.

Schleiermacher was the first theologian who, under the influence of contemporary philosophy,

27

made a systematic attempt to explain Christian truth by an analysis of the laws and natural conditions of the religious consciousness. To be sure, in his personal piety, Schleiermacher discriminated thoroughly between a transcendent fact and his human effort to explain and discuss that fact. But in adapting Christian facts to the conditions of the scientific thinking of his generation, he established, along with the original principle of the Reformation, a second constitutive principle for Christian theology. Revelation *and* religious consciousness, taken as constituent principles of Christian theology, are quite as dangerous a combination as is that of religion *and* reason, so characteristic of the critical and idealistic philosophy of the time. Danger arises as soon as the truth becomes obscured that there are not two co-ordinated, equally valid principles in Christianity, but that revelation is the unique and fundamental fact, which enters secondarily into relationship with reason and affects the religious consciousness.

A process was thus inaugurated at the beginning of the nineteenth century whereby, as Harnack has said, the Christian religion was placed in the circle of the other objects of human cognition, and the attempt was made to describe its reality and truth according to universally valid historical, psychological and theoretical principles of cognition. The secularization of the religion of revelation was begun. This meant nothing less than its replacement by a religion of human culture, or a revival of the old *theologia naturalis*, which had held a subordinate place even in the theology of the Reformation. A philosophic and cultural element had entered into the field of Christian thinking. It continued to be a characteristic element of all idealistic, liberal and modernistic theology throughout the last century, and, in what has been called on the Continent the "modern-positive" theology, it even penetrated the conservative position.

It must be said that this harmonization of the *scandalum* of revelation with human reason, which was similar to the former harmonization of human reason with cosmic law in German Idealism, was attempted in the interest of a more effective proclamation of the Gospel to the world. The apologetic aim was to present the facts of revelation in terms of normal human thinking. Taking his point of departure from the facts of the religious consciousness rather than from the fact of revelation, it was quite consistent for Schleiermacher, the father of theological modernism, to go on to define the Church as a fellowship which exists as a natural result of human action, or as a fellowship based on piety. Where Christian theology is founded on the data of Christian experience, the Church is not the result of a creative act of God, but is simply the fruit of pious human effort.

Schleiermacher has exerted an influence on Protestant theology which cannot be overestimated. Revelation as an historical act of God was, of course, not eliminated from Christian thinking; it was considered an objective fact entering human thinking. Even by positive or pietistic theology it was regarded as a fact of which human thinking could dispose in the same way as it disposes of other objective elements of human culture. In this respect there is little difference to-day between the tendencies of modernistic theology represented, for instance, by Biedermann, Lipsius and Wendt, and those of a more conservative theology like that of Frank. The consequence of this juxtaposition of principles, most interesting for our times, can be seen in the theology of Richard Rothe, who identified the Church with the State, and predicted that in the future the Church would be dissolved in the State, since the State would become so Christianized as to assume the functions of the Church. Present-day Germany did not seem very far from such a conception a few months ago, when State commissioners took over the control of Church affairs.

It mattered little if, instead of *religion and reason*, or *religion and Christian consciousness*, a more modern combination of principles was attempted in the theology of Ritschl. The effort there was to harmonize the Christian message with the cultural ethos of the time. *Revelation and ethos* gives a synthesis which again excludes the uniqueness of the constituent principles of Christian thinking established by the Reformation. In this effort the attempt was made, in accordance with the empirical spirit of the time, to avoid metaphysical utterances and to confine theology to the *fides qua creditur*, neglecting the *fides quae creditur*. The question of Christian truth, which is the fundamental question of Christian theology, was largely neglected. This pessimistic turning away from truth was the consequence of a loss of courage: man no longer dared to base Christian theology on a sovereign act of God transcending all human capacity of understanding, and, therefore, all possible rationalization in concepts of cultural thinking.[1]

Continental Protestant theology, therefore, for the last hundred years, has been a desperate struggle between a defensive army representing the genuine theology of the Reformation and the liberal and modernist or pietist schools. The theology of the latter has seemed to be more interested in a synthesis of Christian truth with elements of modern culture and thinking, or in the adaptation of the faith to the conditions of our inner life, than in a clear and courageous exposition of the fundamental facts of revelation.

Some forty years ago Adolf von Harnack published a most illuminating book on the nature of Christianity, which was quite characteristic of this effort to make the transcendent facts of revelation intelligible to the ordinary human mind. The facts of the life and death of our Saviour were reduced to certain general truths and to the declaration that the person of Christ was not essential to the Christian message as preached by Jesus.

Pietism, widely spread throughout the Continental Churches, did not solve the problem of Christian truth, but seemed to be satisfied with the mystical and pious experiences of the spiritual life, and

[1] See Karl Barth's *Dogmatics*, I.

tended to dismiss the idea of the Christian Church as guardian of the truth of revelation.

The final consequence of this evolution was the theology of Ernst Troeltsch, and his effort to find a religious *a priori* in human nature which should justify the Christian message before the tribunal of human reason—an effort which led finally to his leaving the theological faculty of Heidelberg, to enter the philosophic faculty of the University of Berlin. Simultaneously a social theology was rising under the leadership of such men as Blumhardt, Kutter and Ragaz. These men considered the question of truth in Christian theology less important than the practical application of the Gospel to modern social problems.

To sum up: before the war, the theology of the Lutheran as well as the Reformed Churches, which form by far the largest block of Protestantism on the Continent, had undergone the neutralizing influence of these modernistic principles—autonomous reason, religious consciousness and cultural ethos. The secularization of the theology of Revelation was complete.

4. THE REBIRTH OF THE SPIRIT OF THE REFORMATION

The war and its aftermath meant a turning-point in this development of Continental theology. Great changes in the souls of men are certainly God's work. Nevertheless, we may ask what secondary causes have contributed to change the Christian mind of Europe. So far as we can see with human eyes, two facts are responsible for the rebirth of the religious life of Europe.

(a) The war meant not only the defeat of an army. It was the defeat of a spirit; it dramatized the limit of man's possibilities. The destruction and suffering which are everywhere to-day to be found in the majority of the Continental countries has had its own deepening influence on the human mind. Great ideals collapsed during the war. Never before has the helplessness of mankind and the futility of human effort become so visible as in the last fifteen years. It is not only the defeated countries which have come to the end of their wealth and means; to all nations the war has meant deprivation, poverty and helplessness. The war did not settle one single human problem. It did not destroy war. It did not make the world safe for democracy. It did not bring peace. It did not create new possibilties for international fellowship and co-operation. Even the peaceful methods of the League of Nations and the International Labour Office, the Economic Conferences and the Disarmament Conference have not been successful in realizing their great ideals. It is as if the spirit and mind of men had lost all power to move and change the world. Neither the military efforts of the armed nations, nor scientific research, nor conference methods have found a way out of the difficulties of the world. No new ideal of the society of man, no social effort, no human sacrifice, no moral idealism has been able to deliver mankind from the scourge of unemployment, the

C

33

economic world crisis, the spirit of hatred and the exclusive nationalism and isolationism which still menaces mankind with disintegration and disaster.

The Churches have been no more successful in their effort to combine forces against the evils which have befallen humanity. The World Alliance for Promoting International Friendship through the Churches has not been able to force the world to renounce warships, submarines and gas bombs; nor has the Universal Christian Council for Life and Work been able to propose a practical solution for unemployment and other burning problems; nor has the World Conference on Faith and Order been able to go very much further than to state wherein the Churches differ from each other.

What has all this meant for the Christian mind which tries to interpret reality in the light of the Bible and to find at least an underlying theory in harmony with Christian ideals? It was quite natural that the peoples facing starvation were much more ready to think through these problems than those who were enjoying prosperity. Human suffering has always educated, has even produced profound thinkers. It is not the first time that a catastrophe has been responsible for a change in the Christian mind. The earthquake of Lisbon, in 1755, shook not only thousands of houses in a large city, but the whole Christian optimism of that time. The war had a similar effect on Christian thinking on the Continent. The vain efforts of militarism to settle man's destiny, the failures of conferences convened for the solution of international problems, all seemed to prove that man had reached his limit: that he was not so strong, nor so wise, nor so good as we had thought; that neither the State, nor the Church, neither human force nor human spirit had really the power to change the world and to assure the life and peace of man. A large part of the European population, having gone through years of vain hoping and unspeakable suffering, fell into the demoniacal pessimism of the Bolshevist revolution which rides rough-shod over the lives of millions of men and over all religious ideals, in order to make way for the redeeming power of a new economic and political system. Other millions, to whom the moral and religious nihilism of Bolshevism was utterly repulsive and impossible, fell into religious pessimism, the precedent for which they discovered in the Bible itself. And here we come to the other reason for the change in the general attitude of the European mind.

Millions of Christian men and women—laymen, professors and ministers—had despaired of man's possibilities. The Christian soul resembled Noah's dove which flew over the waters and, finding nowhere a resting-place, flew back to the ark. The Christian soul of the Continent, finding no support in the world, turned again towards God, the only help, and found Him again in the Bible. It discovered there the Biblical conception of the world's opposition to God; it began again to conceive of the world as the place of suffering, the object of God's wrath and judgment. A new understanding of the eschatological meaning of the New Testa-

35

ment, of the Gospel of Jesus and of the Apocalyptic hope in the last book of the Bible made its way into Christian theology. Young and prosperous people had not counted on the end of the world as the Bible describes it. But poor and starving people who could no longer live in this world, who saw their children dying and their life possibilities wrecked, were prepared to listen to the eschatological message of the Prophets, who taught their people to accept the end of the world, or at least of their nation, as God's will. The dear and loving Father in Heaven seemed to have hidden His face: the neighbourly God of the former era became the *Deus absconditus*, the terrible and hidden God, the *Deus numinosus*, to whom Professor Otto had pointed and of whom Luther himself had so often spoken.

(*b*) The world was becoming narrower and narrower—and less and less intelligible; but the Bible was opened again and in it the essential relationship of God and man was again discovered. The armies had formerly implored God for victory; now the despairing people had to learn the lesson of the Prophets, that not victory but utter defeat and judgment may be the will of God.

In the midst of all the modernistic theories the Bible had continued to live; and with it lived its conception of the world, its eschatological message of the end of this world and the coming of God's Kingdom, its emphasis on God's sovereignty, on the presence of the Spirit, on revelation, on judgment and salvation. Now the old message of the Bible was realized in a new way, in the midst of a doomed world.

Theology began to lay a fresh emphasis on the old Bible. It was clear that modern criticism had been helpful in explaining the *milieu* of the Biblical writers; but the deeper meaning of the Holy Word was not necessarily discovered when the linguistic conditions and historical and psychological interpretations were elucidated. The Word of God does not necessarily speak to man and touch his conscience when an accurate scientific interpretation of the text is given. With the breaking down of a general worldly culture and a cultural theology, theology itself became more scriptural and more humble, inspired with the real desire to listen first to the word of God before interpreting it in scientific terms, to bow under its Divine command before systematizing it in Christian doctrine.

With this acknowledgment of the first formal principle of the Reformation—justification by faith —the Bible as the sole source of Christian knowledge was rediscovered for contemporary Protestantism. The imperative character of God's revelation was again emphasized, and any theology of impartial scientific theologians became suspect. Christian theology remembered again that it stands and falls with the theology of revelation, that the point of departure must be God's Word and action, first of all in Christ—and not first of all in any quality of human consciousness. The fact was again emphasized that revelation is not the result of the historic evolution of the religious consciousness of man, that no continuity between God and man can be admitted, but that revelation is the free act of God, giving a new start to human history. The only human fact corresponding to revelation is faith. A whole generation rediscovered again what it means to live by faith—not by speculation, not by scientific argument, not by sweet Christian experience or mystical meditation, but only by the faith which God gives. In faith man is *von oben geöffnet* (opened from above), so that God's sovereignty in all matters of salvation is maintained, even in the act of faith, which is not a human effort and not even the finest flower of Christian experience.

The rediscovery of this great truth meant a rebirth of the spirit of the Reformation. It involved an immediate attack on the ruling tendencies in modern liberal theology. Emil Brunner declared such an attack a necessary task for Biblical theology and claimed for *eristic* controversial theology a special place in theological studies. This struggle, which has already lasted for nearly twenty years, is not so much directed against Biblical criticism, which knows its own limits, as against three leading tendencies in modern theology.

(1) It is directed, first, against the humanistic point of departure in modernistic theology, or against that Christian Cartesianism which found such a powerful interpreter in Schleiermacher.[1] Neither the Neo-Calvinistic nor the Neo-Lutheran theologies accept any longer Christian consciousness as the basis of Protestant theology. This theology

[1] See Emil Brunner, *die Mystik und das Wort*, T. C. B. Mohr, Tübingen.

cannot be built upon the data of human experience
—neither upon individual experience nor the general
Christian experience of a generation or of Christian
culture as a whole. Theology cannot take its origin
from anthropology. A merely anthropological conception of the spirit and the revealed facts of
Christianity reduces Christendom to a mere element
of culture, and confines it to historic evolution.

Wherever Christian experience or the quality
of Christian consciousness are taken as points of
departure, the temptation exists for Christian
theology to develop these data of the human mind
into an idealistic and autonomous system. Christian
idealism then becomes the competitor of the
Christian theology of revelation. The "dialectic
theology" of Karl Barth and Emil Brunner, therefore, directs its strongest attacks against the idealism
which, in its undeniably high spiritual and moral
qualities, has hitherto been identified with the best
of the Christian spirit. Idealism is the natural fruit
of the philosophy of Descartes, who based existence
on the fact of human thinking, and of the Kantian
philosophy and its principle of the autonomy of
reason. In the philosophy of Fichte and Hegel,
a complete identification took place between the
principle of human reason and the absolute spirit.
In Hegel's philosophy of history the process of
revelation and redemption was reduced to the
logical evolution of the absolute spirit in its three-
fold rhythm of thesis, antithesis and synthesis. The
absolute spirit became conscious of itself in religious
thinking. Even where the philosophical form of this

39

idealism had little influence on Christian thinking, the whole idealistic and autonomous conception of spiritual life which it fostered, consciously or unconsciously, influenced Christian theology.

Professor Spranger, the great philosopher of education, at the University of Berlin, declares, for instance, that Christian faith must be prepared to defend its truth before the tribunal of reason. Holl, the great explorer of the mind of Luther, states that nothing should be recognized as religious except what can be found in present reality and what can be reproduced out of our own human experience. Such idealistic autonomy and Christian Cartesianism is recognized to-day to be in contradiction to a Christian theology based on the fact of Divine revelation. Where human reasoning claims to be the criterion for the value and truth of religious fact, the Holy Spirit has been replaced by the human spirit. A philosophical, moral and secular element has taken the place of God's claim *upon*, and God's Word *to* men. This cultural Protestantism of to-day is under indictment and is being openly attacked as the modern Protestant heresy.

(2) The second tendency in modernistic theology which is under the heavy fire of the regenerated theology of the Reformation is the quality of self-certainty and self-assurance. Where certainty of faith is based on certainty of experience, a fallacious and unchristian assurance clouds the Christian mind. Certainty of God and of salvation then reduces itself to a self-certainty of logical thinking or a self-evidence of human experience, which is

entirely different from the certainty of faith. Wobbermin, for instance, declares that the experience
of the ego represents the surest certainty of reality
and that it is the real basis for all judgments dealing
with the reality of the exterior world. This false
human religious certainty is being attacked to-day
as incompatible with the certainty which is based,
not on human data, but on God's Word. In this
respect Neo-Calvinistic and Neo-Lutheran theologians are attacking not only modernistic theology,
but also conservative theology, which interprets
Christian truth as an objective statement, similar
to and of the same certainty as scientific fact. The
truth of faith cannot be compared with the truth
discovered by scientific research. The latter kind
of truth can be handled by the human mind as an
objective element of which we can dispose according
to our human laws of reasoning. We shall see later
how the Neo-Calvinistic and Neo-Lutheran attack
on such a fallacious certainty is also directed against
that American fundamentalism which confounds
certainty of faith with scientific certainty. In the
conservative Lutheran and Calvinistic theology of
the Continent we sometimes encounter an easy
spirit of certainty which is little short of disrespect
towards God as *actus purus*, as the freely disposing
power who elects and condemns; reveals and veils
Himself; acts or remains passive, according to His
own inscrutable freedom. A heavy attack is, therefore, being directed against the self-assurance of
Christian humanists as well as against the static
certainty of those who deal with the Divine promises

41

as elements of a theological system and not as the free acts of a Divine Will, of which we by no means have the disposal. This rediscovery of God's sovereignty is an important aspect of that rebirth of the spirit of the Reformation of which we have spoken. Certainty of faith is not identical with power over God's initiative. Professor Althaus said once: "I am not sure whether I really believe, but I know in Whom I believe."

(3) The third tendency in present-day theology which is being attacked by Neo-Calvinism and Neo-Lutheranism is the attempt—a natural consequence of idealism—to find a synthesis between the Divine and the human spirit. From the days of Idealism on, a monistic tendency has been observed in the desire of theology to justify itself before rational science, where Christian faith is considered merely the finest flower of the human spirit or the best possible synthesis between God's spirit and that of man. Confusion has obscured our knowledge of the clear original Christian fact of revelation. With the contemporary rebirth of the Reformation, the difference between God and man, between revelation and faith, between the human ego and God's holy personality, between the God of our consciousness and the God of heaven and earth, is being emphasized afresh. On the Lutheran side, Professor Elert stresses the necessity of such a *diastasis*, such a differentiation. He deprecates the former tendency to look for a synthesis between God and man, God's deed and human experience. When the followers of the Lutheran, Holl, claim a hidden identity between

the Divine and the human in the act of faith, their position is attacked as irreverent and untrue—God being in heaven, and man on earth. Nobody has been more uncompromising in claiming an essential difference between the Divine and the human logos than Karl Barth. He attacks any synthesis with utmost severity. Be it the attempt to combine revelation and reason, revelation and religious consciousness, revelation and cultural ethos or revelation and religious history, he condemns the "and," between two such irreconcilable facts, as utterly opposed to the spirit of the Reformation and its claim for the sovereignty of God. He attacks even the title of the latest book of his friend, Emil Brunner, *Das Gebot und die Ordnungen.* Christian theology must begin not with such a synthesis but with a complete recognition of the sovereignty of God and of His grace.[1]

The revival of the original Reformed doctrine of the sovereignty of God parallels the rebirth of the spirit of the Reformation. It is true that this renaissance had been anticipated by theologians of a conservative character in various countries. Professor Kaehler and Professor Schlatter in Germany had never ceased to protest against the modernistic theology. Professor Heim in Tübingen, Professor Seeberg in Berlin, and Professor Althaus in Erlangen, have tried in recent years to present the whole Protestant position in a new form to a new generation. In Holland the Orthodox

[1] Emil Brunner has answered in a significant brochure, *Natur und Gnade* (*Nature and Grace*), Mohr, Tübingen, touching here not only the schism in the theology of crisis, but also the old controversy between Catholicism and Protestantism.

Calvinistic theology, represented by Mr. Kuyper, President of the Dutch Government, had founded a new Church, the *Gereformeerde Kerk*, protesting against the modernistic spirit in the European Churches. This little Church has established an independent university at Amsterdam, and has developed remarkable activity, born of the new inspiration. Even in liberal theology, men like Herrmann in Marburg and Wobbermin in Göttingen had begun years ago to protest against the claims of the historian and the psychologist. They placed the living Christ in the centre of their teaching, in spite of the fact that they did not yet clearly see that the three tendencies of which I have spoken are a menace to the spirit of the Reformation.

Continental theology is far from having attained homogeneity. The present theological situation must be described as a struggle. The old slogans, orthodox and liberal, are no longer valid, because deeper final questions have been put before both of these parties by the recent Neo-Calvinistic and Neo-Lutheran theologies. They will be dealt with later. It is a matter of gratification to see that in this struggle the great fundamental facts of revelation are no longer discussed as mere elements in a conflict of theological parties, but are regarded as essential questions in our relationship with God. It is felt that the attitude of Christians towards these facts will decide whether, in the midst of a world where humanity seems to be engaged in a final struggle for or against God, the Church of Christ is or is not to be.

III

NEO-CALVINISM AND NEO-LUTHERANISM

THE birth of the spirit of the Reformation which was described in the last chapter cannot be regarded as being a discovery by a single theologian or by any special school of theological thought. Nor is it confined either to Calvinism or to Lutheranism alone. It is a general movement cutting across these two large groups of Churches which historically represent Continental Protestantism. The new theology is not a peculiarity of Karl Barth in Bonn, or Professor Brunner in Zürich, or Professor Lecerf in Paris, or Professor Haitjema in Holland, or Professors Aulén and Runestam in Sweden. Nor is it a wave of personal religious life, the effect of the need and suffering of the time. It should not be misinterpreted as being merely war or post-war theology. It is rather a new consideration of what God has said and is always saying in His Word. If we describe the movement as Neo-Calvinism or Neo-Lutheranism, we must keep in mind the fact that something has come alive in Continental theology which is not simply a repetition of the old Calvinistic or Lutheran thought forms.

Before trying to give a survey of this movement, which is in evidence in Lutheran quite as much as in Calvinistic Churches, we ought perhaps to review briefly the relationship which has existed between Lutheranism and Calvinism in the last decades.

1. THE SCHISM OF THE REFORMATION AND ITS ECCLESIASTICAL RESULTS

On the occasion of the Diet of Marburg, in 1529, Landgrave Philip of Hesse tried to reconcile Luther and Zwingli, perhaps with a view to common political action. Luther and Zwingli failed to establish a final agreement, although they reached a common understanding on fourteen points. In discussing the fifteenth, the doctrine of the Holy Communion, the deeper differences between the two reformers came to light. The conference broke off with the attempt of Zwingli to extend a fraternal hand to Luther and the refusal of the latter to accept it. Luther's words were harsh: *"Yours is a different spirit from ours."* Recent research by Professor Walter Köhler in Heidelberg has shown that it was, perhaps, not Luther alone who was responsible for what seemed to be an unfraternal act; also that the two reformers were nearer together in the essentials than they themselves knew.

Nevertheless, these unfortunate words were not forgotten, and the unfriendly gesture remained, so to speak, as the fixed symbol of a permanent schism between Lutheranism and the Reformed Churches.

The first official expression of this unhappy schism in the Reformation was put in dogmatic form in the *Confessio Augustana*, in 1530. The first edition of this great *symbolum*, the *Augustana invariata*, sharply condemned the principles of the Reformed

46

Church and subsequently prevented a union between the Lutheran and the Reformed bodies. Only much later a kind of union was achieved in the Prussian Church by Frederick William III. It was not a confessional, but only an administrative union. The two confessions were equally recognized in it and lived peacefully together under the same roof, the same consistory, the same Church law, the same *summus episcopus*—which title the king assumed for himself. This union satisfied neither the Lutheran nor the Reformed bodies and was opposed with special vehemence by the Lutherans outside of Prussia. Even in Prussia a considerable group of "Old Lutherans" refused to enter it and continued to maintain the reserved and condemning attitude of the *Augustana invariata*. No other attempt at such a union was made anywhere in the rest of Europe, except in the Church of the Czech brethren and recently in the Evangelical Church in Austria.

2. PRACTICAL CO-OPERATION BETWEEN LUTHERANS AND REFORMED

Nevertheless, practical necessity compelled the two groups to live and work together in various countries. Where doctrine was not made an issue, it became possible for the Lutheran and Reformed Churches to collaborate in joint foreign and home missionary organizations. Church federations were formed including Lutheran and Reformed bodies. The "Central European Bureau for Inter-Church Aid" was founded, in 1922, on a common inter-denominational basis. The "Society for the Defence of Protestantism" had a similar foundation. In recent œcumenical movements Lutheran and Reformed leaders have learned to grapple jointly with urgent social problems; and in the "Faith and Order Movement" a fresh beginning has been made in the discussion even of theological questions. The Conference on Faith and Order at Lausanne, in 1927, showed very distinctly that a common evangelical front already existed between the Lutheran and Reformed Churches, in so far as both stood for the great principles of the Reformation, namely, the spiritual interpretation of the meaning of grace, the universal priesthood of believers, and religious freedom. The Church conflict in Germany has again strengthened practical co-operation on a common front on matters of Church politics.

3. THE FREE CHURCHES

The so-called "free" Churches on the Continent, mostly of the Methodist, Baptist or Moravian type, although numerically weak, are of great spiritual importance and exert a strong missionary influence, despite the fact that in certain countries these free Churches do not even enjoy legal existence. In Austria, Jugo-Slavia, and Poland, the State has recognized only the Lutheran and Reformed Confessions, so that no other group has a legal standing. In Italy the free missionary Churches do not enjoy the same privileges as the Catholic Church, or even those of the Waldensian faith.

It seemed for a while as if a large missionary field

48

were opening in the east of Europe, especially in Russia, for the Methodist and, more especially, the Baptist Churches, both of which have a more aggressive missionary spirit than the old national Lutheran and Reformed bodies. The Russian Revolution, however, has arrested these movements. The whole relationship of the free Churches to the recognized and strong Lutheran and Reformed communions on the Continent, especially in modern Germany, is an unsolved problem. The revolution in Germany may, in the long run, strengthen the principle of "free Churches," although the legal standing of the existing ones is not yet assured. As these are mostly of foreign origin and have their central boards outside of the Continent, we shall confine our study mostly to the native Churches of the Lutheran and Reformed type.

4. A NEW SPIRIT IN LUTHERANISM

In both Church groups the rebirth of the spirit of the Reformation has taken the form of a strengthening of the denominational consciousness. This, however, should be understood primarily as a common desire to rediscover and reinterpret the great fundamental truths of the evangelical faith which broke forth in the Reformation. A great effort has been made during the last twenty years to understand the real meaning of the Reformation and to liberate the reformers' theology, as well as their theories of Church government, from incidental characteristics—that is, from their implication in the religious psychology and political situation of their time. The anniversary of the Reformation, in the midst of the war, 1917, illustrated this endeavour. A large number of publications showed that a new interest in Luther, especially in Luther as a youth, had awakened. This led to new discoveries. But every discovery involves a personal interpretation which may be denied by the next generation. Professor Holl at the University of Berlin, for example, certainly inaugurated a new understanding of Luther; but the interpretation of the present generation has already attacked it as being too subjective and too greatly influenced by the ideals of modernism and cultural Protestantism. The present Lutheran interpreters of Luther and the Lutheran Reformation, such as Professors Aulén and Runestam in Sweden, Professors Althaus, Elert and Sasse in Erlangen—partly under the influence of Karl Barth—are trying to avoid such modernistic or liberal influences in their interpretation of the young Luther. At the present time they are making a great effort to protect their "hero" from a modern National Socialist (Nazi) interpretation. We shall deal with this problem in a later lecture.

The leading interpreters of Luther have certainly discovered new aspects of this divinely endowed personality. As against Roman Catholic interpretations, such as those of the German Jesuits, Denifle and Grisar, and the French writer Maritain, a fresh emphasis was laid on the exclusiveness of grace and faith, in the evangelical conception of Christian life. Other aspects of Luther's theology

NEO-CALVINISM AND NEO-LUTHERANISM

were better understood in the light of newly discovered personal experiences of the reformer. We understand better to-day, for example, what the *Deus absconditus*, the hidden God, meant for Luther. This hidden God was not so easily accessible as the "loving Father" of sentimental tradition, but was adored and feared by Luther as the majestic and sovereign God whose world plans cannot easily be understood in nature, in history, or in personal destiny. He is the *Deus numinosus*, the *mysterium tremendum ac fascinosum* of which Professor Otto speaks in his book, *The Idea of the Holy*—the unknown and transcendent God who is a consuming fire, and whose love we see nowhere else than in the face of Christ.

The wrath of God is also a feature of this new interpretation of the theology of Luther. What grace means is better understood against the dark and terrible background of the wrath of that God who is our supreme Judge and Lord. The positive pedagogical religious meaning of law, of the State and the Church, is rediscovered especially by Swedish Lutherans.

This new spirit in Lutheranism is perhaps more conspicuous in Swedish Lutheranism than in German. In the latter a new nationalistic or racial theology was a stronger temptation to certain Lutheran theologians than to those of the Reformed faith. Swedish Lutherans like Nygren and Runestam, standing firmly on the doctrine of "Justification by Faith," have successfully defended the genuine Luther against a modern form of Lutheranism.

51

COLUMBIA BIBLE COLLEGE LIBRARY
Columbia, S. C.
20667

Even where the old doctrinal formulae are used, it is evident that they are filled with a new spirit, a readiness to acknowledge the spiritual authority of the Bible, in spite of Biblical criticism, to take a fresh stand on grace alone, to mark the difference between God's transcendent and coming kingdom and this aeon which is under His judgment,[1] and to build up an ethics, long neglected by the former Lutheranism, not on a philosophical but on the truly evangelical basis of justification by faith and on a new discrimination between the reign of Grace and the reign of the world.

5. A RENAISSANCE OF REFORMED THEOLOGY

The "dialectical" theology of Karl Barth, Emil Brunner, E. Thurneysen and de Quervain represents the reawakening of the spirit of the Reformation in the Reformed ranks. This movement has now had wide repercussions in most of the Continental Churches, especially in Germany, Switzerland, Holland, Denmark, and Hungary. Dialectical theology, as the system of thought associated with Karl Barth is generally called, is the strongest of the tendencies taking modern Protestantism back towards a rediscovery of the genuine truth of the Reformation. We must, therefore, enter more deeply into its main features and

[1] We have to refer here to the works of Elert (*Morphologie des Luthertums*) Althaus, Aulén, Nygren, Runestam. But the strategic position in the present struggle is held by Reformed theologians with whom we deal in the next chapter.

[2] Cf. my *Karl Barth and Christian Unity*, Lutterworth Press, London, 1934.

meaning. In it, present-day Neo-Calvinism has reached a culminating point.

(a) *The Meaning of the Barthian Theology*

When, in 1909, Karl Barth began preaching in the *Auditoire*, where Calvin gave his theological lessons and John Knox also preached for several years, nobody was aware that he was to become a regenerator of Calvinistic theology, although one felt the unusual power of his spirit, his intransigence in theological thinking and his intrepidity and aggressiveness towards the world as it was. He later became pastor of Safenwil in Switzerland. He has left us a record of the spiritual distress in which he found himself as a preacher being confronted with an historical theology which reduced the Gospel to what was historically provable, a religious psychology which tried to make it palatable to ordinary human experience and a moralism characteristic of bourgeois circles which confined it to a system of moral principles. He had no use for this modernistic and liberal, or merely moral, interpretation. But, on the other hand, he was confronted with a Christian conservatism which understood the facts of revelation as given historical data—that is to say, as so much Divine capital consisting of transcendent facts and ethical commandments which had become the property of men and which they could treat in the same way as the facts and laws of a scientific system. This kind of Christianity felt itself to be in complete possession of salvation. In its false fundamentalist assurance it had forgotten the dynamic character of God's revelation, which lifts the Gospel beyond the possibility of being permanently posited by human experience and Christian knowledge.

To Barth, as a Christian Socialist, it seemed that the Church was lacking in social courage to seek new manifestations of God's Spirit. He was stimulated, first, by Christoph Blumhardt, a pietist in Württemberg, who had become an official member of the Social Democratic party in Germany, and second, by Pastor Kutter in Zürich, who interpreted Socialism as a kind of unconscious Christianity, standing for the ideal of social justice, human solidarity and the fraternal fellowship of men under a high altruistic guiding principle. Another influence came from the Danish philosopher, Kierkegaard, whose thought is now one of the most active elements in the revolutionized Christian life of the Continent. This teacher emphasized the necessity for the individual to undertake personal responsibility in the great adventure of the new life with God, and not to be afraid to stand alone. Karl Barth discovered a final critical influence in the theology of Professor Overbeck of Basle, who denied the Christian character of a Christendom which had made its peace with the world. He saw the original spirit of the Gospel in an ascetic and unworldly love of poverty and in an eschatological belief in the end of this world.

While under these influences, Karl Barth had to meet not only a shallow immanentism in religion, coupled with a mild and defensive conservatism, but also the rising aggressive spirit of such new religions as Communism, Fascism and "Americanism" (as optimistic capitalism had come to be called on the Continent), and he was aware of the danger of any compromise which would betray Christendom to these new religions of national, racial, material and cultural interests. He asked, therefore, "Is our Christianity still Christianity?" and held that it was such only when man listens and God speaks in His eternal message of Christ. True Christian experience begins always "with hearing and renewed hearing and better hearing."

What are we to hear? The Word of God which is Jesus Christ.

This was the new appeal which Karl Barth made in his first book, *The Epistle to the Romans*, which is now available in an English translation by Sir Edwin Hoskyns. It was a message with a prophetic character, partly exegetical, partly devotional, but mainly expressing a new spiritual attitude towards the Bible. Since publishing this great book, Barth has attempted to systematize his method of approach in a theological system, his *Dogmatics*, of which the first volume appeared in 1927 and again, altered from cover to cover, in 1932. The latter was indeed a totally new volume —and an equally new *Dogmatics*. There are many theologians who regret this transformation of a spiritual, prophetic message into a dogmatic system, which is interpreted by many as simply a repetition of old orthodox positions. But Karl Barth feels the obligation, as a theologian, to listen for and obey God's command and express it in terms of human thinking.

As against all theology of the religious consciousness, or of ethical or mystical experience, or of philosophical reflection and speculation, Karl Barth's is a theology of the Word.

What is God's Word? It has a three-fold meaning. It is, first, the Word *as preached*. As such, it has an imperative character. God's Word is not simply a communication or an objective statement, but a positive command which does not permit man to assume the attitude of a spectator or to enjoy mere disinterested research. It is a motive which is not given as a datum of consciousness or of any human experience whatsoever. It is not subject to our power, but is effective whenever, wherever and however it wills. Even preachers of the Word are only receivers. In so far as they receive it, it becomes an object for their vision and experience. The Divine Word then, indeed, becomes a human word, but only on the basis of our recognition of the Divine primacy. The human Word is a Divine announcement only in so far as the Divine Word is actually and simultaneously expressed by it. God's Word in human speech, therefore, is not a given article of knowledge, not a self-sustaining truth, nor an independent judgment. It is spoken, however, whenever Christ makes His entrance into the human situation, that is, specifically, in all the historical and individual acts in which the world has been, and still is, confronted by the presence of the living Christ. Karl Barth would be willing to accept a doctrine of apostolic succession whereby Christ is conceived as being present in His human vicars, provided that the succession humbly and obediently represented Christ and did not replace His authority by an authority of its own, as happens in the Roman Catholic Church.

The second form of God's Word is the written Word, the Holy Scripture. This is God's Word in that it is a memory of a past revelation of God and an expectation of future revelation. The Church possesses a written Word, a canon of Holy Scripture, but the autonomy and independence of the Word of God in relationship to the Church is not thereby jeopardized. God's Word remains a free power and a living revelation of what God has done and will do. This prevents the Church from identifying itself, its experiences and its tradition, with God's Word. It forbids the Church from claiming to be herself the Word of God, or from speaking with the authority of God. It keeps her in the position of one who is addressed by an external and superior authority.

From this point of view, Karl Barth is strongly opposed to any canonized interpretation of the Bible, which defines once for all the meaning of the Word of God and prevents the Holy Spirit from using the written Word as a manifestation of God's will. When the Church tries to define once and for ever what the authoritative interpretation of the Bible should be, it assumes an authority which it does not possess and identifies itself with the dynamic action of the Spirit. Karl Barth demands a free exegesis of the Bible, trusting in the spiritual power of the Word of God to explain itself and to remain eternally a critical, corrective power over against any man's purely individualistic interpretation of it. To any man in a truly listening and obedient attitude, the Bible explains itself. It is for ever giving fresh evidence of itself as being the voice of the revealing God—a God who speaks to us not in established interpretative formulas, in dead letters, but in an actual and dynamic Word which becomes, through the action of the Holy Spirit, a personal and ever renewed event. When we call the Bible the Word of God, we are not referring to the human interpretation of God's Word, but only to the act of faith by which we believe in the God who speaks in the Bible wherever, whenever and through whatever words He will.

The third form is the Word *as revealed*. Revelation is the prior and fundamental act; the Bible is its witness. The latter should not be identified with revelation, therefore. The Bible points towards revelation, and revelation always happens in and through the Word of God in the written Bible; but the Bible itself should not be identified with revelation.

In this theology the Word of God is understood as the fundamental, dynamic and ever-present element to which we have to listen in an attitude of obedience before we can assimilate it in our human experience or knowledge, or explain it by human comment. This conception is as much opposed to a humanistic and modernistic interpretation, which treats the Bible as an assemblage of mere historical and psychological facts, as it is to that conservative conception which treats it as a datum, a static entity which can be classified by the human mind.

The dialectic theology is therefore a real theology of revelation. This is to say that our knowledge of God comes from God and not from a religious *a priori*, not from the alleged original religious nature of man, nor the capacities of his religious consciousness, nor his mystical experiences. God is in heaven, man on earth. Between God and man the same qualitative difference exists as between time and eternity, though to-day Karl Barth would no longer base this discrimination on a philosophic idea, as he did in former years. In opposition to every theology of immanence which tries to discover God in the given nature of the human soul, he stresses the transcendent character of the God who remains the *Deus absconditus*, the hidden, the Unknown God, as long as He does not reveal Himself. A large part of our theological work has been based on immanentist presuppositions. To these the modern mind has everywhere been inclined. Barth attacks even Rudolf Otto and his irrational conception of God as the *numinosum*, and rejects it on the ground that the mere *mysterium tremendum ac fascinosum* cannot be distinguished from any mysterious natural power. God remains the sovereign personality, who has left in our hands not a finished and exhaustive revelation, as is held in the Roman Catholic doctrine of the *ana-*

logia entis—as if analogy between Divine and human existence were possible—but a revelation towards which man must reach.

Revelation for Barth remains a sovereign, divine, dynamic act. What is revealed is not a system, is not God's unfathomable mystery, is not a *fait accompli*, but the action of God as sovereign. Revelation is always the self-revelation of the undiscoverable God.

What does this involve? It involves, first of all, a criticism of any static conception of revelation—whether it is found in conservative or in modernist theology. Such a conception envisages revelation as an accomplished and objective fact, whereby God's mystery is more or less delivered into the hands of man. The Christian then knows what God is, what God means, and what His mystery is. All this is fully revealed and accessible to Christian experience and human thinking. Karl Barth substitutes for such a static conception of revelation a dynamic faith wherein the freedom and the sovereignty of God are safeguarded. God's mystery remains mystery except where, by an act of God, the veil is lifted. But this is never done in such a way that man can control the revealed God or His revealed mystery. There is no "no man's land" between God and humanity which by revelation has become everybody's land. Barth would not say God is revealed once and for all, but that from time to time He reveals Himself. Barth lays every stress on revelation as a free and sovereign act of God Himself.

In the appearance of Christ, in whom the Christian believes he has grasped God's mystery, we are still face to face with a hidden God; else the ordinary man, the pagan in the modern world, would be struck by the fact of the revelation. If the revelation of God in Christ were inescapable, even the Christian would be affected quite differently by the fact of Christ's life and death and resurrection, which so often leaves him utterly quiet, comfortable and unchanged.

Even in Christ, and in the manifestation of His Spirit, God is not delivered to man as an axiom, as a principle, as a clearly definable fact. God's will or Christ's will may, therefore, appear different to different generations and different persons. God's mystery is safeguarded. When "prohibition" was inaugurated in America, many Christians were quite clear about the will of God, thus easily defined in a social programme and in consequent political action. It would be interesting for Barthians on the other side of the ocean to know whether to-day American Christianity is still so very sure about this revealed will of God. The terrible religious experience which we all underwent during the war gave us a new understanding of the Hidden God who does not enter so manifestly into our Christian conceptions, into our ethical or social programmes, or into our static interpretation of His revelation.

Karl Barth would remind many a sincere Christian that this figure which he calls his dear Lord and Saviour—*my* Christ—looks very dangerously like a function of his own instinctive desires. This makes of Christ only what the soul can understand of Him; and the soul is then deceived by its own image of Christ, which is without authority. Are not these liberties which Christians take with God mere attempts to penetrate the mystery which He has reserved to Himself? God's sovereign transcendence was not immanent in the life of Jesus in the sense that it became a tangible, measurable event and a palpable historic fact. Even in the revelation of Christ no general idea of God is revealed, no valid and demonstrable idea; no Divine existence accessible to theological or historical or psychological research. Even there God remains the free sovereign who reveals Himself as the present and Unknown God to *whom* He will and *when* He will.

Revelation must, therefore, be contemplated under three aspects: a veiling, an unveiling and a real intercourse between God and man. Barth finds these three aspects taught by the Church as the several functions of Father, Son, and Holy Ghost.

One is sometimes inclined to think that Barth has forgotten, in this connection, the importance of the doctrine of creation. The publication of his *Dogmatik* is not yet sufficiently advanced to show the relation in its theology between creation and redemption. We must, therefore, rely on former publications to understand his ideas on the subject.

One thing is clear: as mortals, living in finite time, we are no longer concerned with the original creation which was contemplated by God and declared to be good. The great and mysterious fact of sin has intervened.

In the fall of man, his whole nature, in its cognitive as well as in its moral and religious aspects, was corrupted. It is this nature which is referred to in the Reformed doctrine, *finitum non capax infiniti*, which is transformed by Barth into *peccator non est capax verbi Dei*. The deep pessimism of the original supralapsarian doctrine of the Reformed faith is apparent here. It is this which is fundamentally incompatible with modern humanistic American optimism, to which Anselm's great criticism would be applied: *nondum considerasti quanti ponderis sit peccatum*. Redemption has to do with the fallen man, and in so far as Christianity means, first of all, the redemption of man, we are meeting here the central facts of Christian life: sin and grace, not creation and its natural laws.

For Christian faith, sin and grace are not two single and separate items, but correlated facts. Grace exists only for the sinner, and we only speak of sin in respect of grace, which is the central meaning of the principal dogma of the Reformation, *justification by faith*. This dogma declares that the sinner is justified by a sovereign act of God through the sacrifice of Jesus Christ. He is saved by a decree of God's judgment alone and not by any merit or synergistic co-operation of man, or by subsequent sanctification. It is the sinner who is justified—*simul justus et peccator*, as Luther says. The process is not that a man by his moral effort and an act of grace ceases to be a *peccator* and becomes justified. This is not only the Catholic conception, but also the temptation to which Arminian Methodism is exposed. The Christian is justified before God as a sinner and must accept this paradox in his faith—a paradox which finds its parallel in the dialectic method of Barthian theology.

The dialectic method in this sense means the process which ensues when an *I* and a *Thou* really meet, when two opposites enter into a tension and when, therefore, two different aspects of a common reality come to light. Sin and grace are two such opposites, so closely interrelated in Christian life that they cannot be separated. The dialectic method is opposed to all merely critical methods —methods of spectators or judges who feel themselves to be above the whole situation. The dialectic method enters into the life situation and reflects a real and desperately responsible conversation between God and the soul.

(b) The Barthians and their Influence

Dialectic theology is represented to-day not only by Barth himself, but by two other Swiss friends of his. Eduard Thurneysen is, perhaps, nearest to his thought and has had a great share in the elaboration of his theology. He applied its principles to actual Church problems as professor of practical theology at the University of Basle and successor to the famous friend of Zwingli, Œcolampadius.

Professor Emil Brunner stands also for the principles of the sovereignty and transcendence of

64

God, and teaches, as does Karl Barth himself, a theology of the Word and of revelation. He was the first to concentrate his attack on the father of modern theology, Schleiermacher,[1] who, after having been considered a real *pater ecclesiae* by orthodox and liberal theologians of the Continent, is to-day in many places called the father of the modernistic and humanistic heresy. Not everybody, however, is convinced that full justice has been done to Schleiermacher. It is felt that there is still something to be said for his point of departure, that is, the religious consciousness, and even for the youthful idealism of his *Addresses on Religion*. When Schleiermacher concentrated on the qualities of the Christian consciousness, he attempted, in the time-honoured fashion of apologetics, to find a common basis for discussing the religious problem with the representatives of the culture of his time. But neither Barth nor Brunner would recognize the right of such apologetics; they would be apprehensive of the danger of a synthesis between the claims of culture and the claims of God, between reason and revelation. Brunner is, therefore, advocating the introduction of a new theological discipline, the *eristic* method, the function of which would be to guard soundness of doctrine and to elaborate religious truth in a dialectical controversy with its opponents. Brunner was also the first dialectician to write a Christian ethics, *Das Gebot und die Ordnungen*.[2] Like Karl

[1] *Die Mystik und das Wort*, Mohr, Tübingen.
[2] An English edition of this great work is in preparation.

Barth, he interprets God's word as imperative, as a commandment which claims full and absolute obedience from man. In this attitude of obedience Christian ethics cannot help attempting to discover what practical regulation, what provisional ordering of society must be adopted to meet the claims of a given situation at a given time. We shall return to this "ethics" when we deal with the present social problems on the Continent.

Another dialectician is Gogarten, Professor in Breslau, who, with Karl Merz, is the only Lutheran theologian of high standing who has accepted the Barthian view in principle. Gogarten has entered very deeply into the question of Christian experience and, following the thought of Martin Buber and Ferdinand Ebner, has discovered that the place where God meets man is in the neighbour, the friend, the wife, the child and the fellow-man. All of these are placed in our way and have claims on us which we must and yet never can fulfil. Every such *Thou* represents a fatal moment in our life when we become guilty. Every *Thou* means a terrible and unrealizable claim laid upon us by the mysterious God. Here we refuse to obey. Here we maintain our own autonomy and self-sufficiency, whereby God's sovereign claim on our whole existence is flouted.

The common denominator of the whole group cannot easily be defined except by the reference to their common emphasis on the absolute claim of God, upon His sovereignty and transcendence, upon His exclusive grace. We have observed considerable difference between the various representatives. Barth, in his *Dogmatik*, has already expressed the suspicion that the exclusion of grace cannot be maintained if any other principle beside that of God's supreme will is established. He would, for example, question the standing of any human orders whatsoever over against the Divine commandment, as outlined in Brunner's "ethics"; and in Gogarten he would deny the claim of any *Thou* beside God alone.

The theology of this group has experienced a repercussion throughout Europe such as hardly any former school has had. The writer's book, *Karl Barth and Christian Unity*,[1] shows the influence of this theology on the various theological schools in other countries. The reaction of these other schools to this theology might be used, so to speak, as a theological sextant to distinguish the actual constellations of thought on the theological horizon. The various controversies of existing theological groups are indeed good indices of the actual religious situation on the Continent. They are even an important feature in the religious battle which is raging at the heart of the German Revolution. Leading ideas which have been forged by this theological group are being used to-day as trenchant weapons in the fight of evangelical Christians in Germany for soundness of doctrine and evangelical liberty. Nearly all present-day problems in theology—missions, social service activity and Church politics

---

[1] *Karl Barth and Christian Unity*, Macmillan, New York, and Lutterworth Press, London, 1933.

—are reflected in this struggle. A theological
tempest is raging on the Continent, and, so far as
Germany is concerned, even when a new phase
seems to have been reached, some new political
situation is likely to arise overnight to test its
fundamental truth. But this struggle is full of hope,
since it is a struggle for truth. No one, not even
those far removed from the battlefield, can remain
indifferent.

Every theological school is confronted to-day
with the question as to whether it has been faithful
to the great heritage of the Reformation; whether
it is teaching the Gospel given by God Himself,
or a man-made gospel of modern culture and
national religion. Even in the various branches of
the practical activity of the Churches the question
arises whether such work is based on sound theological principles or whether it is merely inspired
by the human will for efficiency, the passion to
organize the world according to the image of man.
The question of evangelical truth is no longer
simply a question for theological parties, but is
the unique and great concern of all theology of the
whole Church. The question regarding truth cannot
be solved by law or by methods of scientific research.
It can be answered only by sound theological
thinking, placed humbly and obediently under the
Word of God.

Yesterday the overwhelming practical activity
of the Church, its manifold interests—in education,
missions and civic and political problems in general
—relegated theology to the background. In certain

Churches and in certain countries theology was considered to be almost superfluous. To-day, at least in Europe, owing largely to the influence of the theology of crisis, theology is again assuming its fundamental and primary task, namely, to proclaim the truth of the Gospel and to test our various human truths in the light of the Divine Truth revealed to us in Jesus Christ.

IV

STORM-CENTRES OF A THEOLOGICAL REVOLUTION

Iᴛ is important to understand that in this rediscovery of certain forgotten truths of the Reformation,
we are dealing not merely with a new theological
school and its controversy with other groups. A
general new orientation in the deeper philosophical and religious life of the Continent is taking
place which is influencing everything—including
theology. It is much more than a controversy
of the schools. It is, in fact, a universal spiritual and
intellectual struggle centring around a new conception of man. During the past century man had
become more and more the centre of thought; his
reason had become identified with world reason;
his human mind was to establish the principles of
the world order. Thinking had the priority over
being. Philosophy was, therefore, predominantly
a philosophy of human consciousness, and was
concerned for the most part with the conditions
of rational cognition.

A radical change has taken place in recent years.
This humanistic philosophy of consciousness or cognition has broken down and has been replaced by a
philosophy of existence, of being. Ontological considerations have re-entered the field of philosophical

studies where hitherto epistemological or psychological interests have had a predominant position. It is a remarkable fact that, at least in Heidegger and Grisebach, the new problems of philosophy have arisen from questions which are essentially theological! What is the place of man? What is his real existence? How can he exist, when on the one side he is tortured by his own questions, and on the other side knows no issue but death, the ultimate and unavoidable reality? Man no longer conceives himself possessed of autonomous reason, lording it in mystical self-sufficiency as king of the world and of thought; he is now the despairing creature who is nothing, who is forlorn, guilty, a sinner and an object of God's wrath. This is the man who receives the miraculous message of God's unconditional grace. This is an astounding announcement and a shock, a *scandalum* to rational thinking. But the new orientation derives from this very announcement which establishes our spiritual existence; this is the centre about which the present struggle is raging.

How can one best give a survey of this battlefield? Perhaps by describing the various fronts on which the spiritual armies are fighting, each for its own interpretation of the central fact accepted by all.

I. THE FIGHT FOR A NEW UNDERSTANDING OF THE REFORMATION

The question is whether the participants in the Neo-Lutheran and Neo-Calvinistic movement—

Althaus, Aulén, Barth, Brunner, Lecerf, and the others—understand the Reformation correctly. The school of Karl Holl, the most influential of modern interpreters of Luther, regards the new interpretation of Luther as quite wrong. Particular objection is raised to the exclusive emphasis which Barth lays on the transcendence of God. Holl interpreted Luther as saying that "the independent conscience is a final element, where God can be found directing the soul towards what is good." The whole moralistic interpretation of the Reformation has its roots here: Luther was interpreted, so to speak, by Immanuel Kant. Luther once compared man to a *larva Dei*, a mask of God. Does this mean that we find God behind a mask of the moral appeal of conscience, and, consequently, in the very essence of human nature as it collaborates with God? Or does it mean that God remains the hidden God, never directly accessible because, even in His revelation, He reveals Himself in this world as veiled? One battlefront is evident here. Holl and his school see in Christ and the Holy Spirit the vital, immanent power by which God imparts the willing and the doing of good. Karl Barth quite as clearly sees the impossibility of any such identification of the sovereign and hidden God with the constituent principle of our spiritual life, and vehemently protests against it. The question is, therefore: Where is the authentic interpretation of the Reformation?

2. IS GOD HIDDEN OR MANIFEST?

An army of theological immanentists is atacking Barth's interpretation of the Reformation from another quarter. They believe his doctrine of the sovereignty of God's grace especially unsound. They regard the Christian experience of a believing Christian as a fact corresponding to an action on God's part, so that, as Wobbermin puts it, a conjunction, a synthesis or a polarity exists between God's Word and man's faith. Wobbermin quotes, for instance, the words of Luther, *Gott und der Glaube gehoeren zu Haufe*—in order to prove that, having received faith, the human consciousness possesses a Divine content which can be examined and studied, capital from God with which the Christian can work. According to this interpretation, there is a synthesis between God's revelation and Christian faith; an identification between the hidden God and God as manifest in our Christian experience. Christian faith as given by God to man, therefore, issues in a monism upon which not only Christian life, but also a Christian theological science can be based.

This position is far from being a mere dispute about the historical explanation of the basic principle of the Reformation—*sola fide* or *soli Deo gloria*. One sees here a serious effort to discover a point of contact for human thinking and experience, to get hold of the Divine promise, the gift of faith, to bring it down from the height of a hope—to bring it down from revelation to the solid ground

73

of a human possession. A large number of Continental theologians like Wobbermin, Schaeder, Winkler, the Scandinavian theologian Torsten Bohlin, the Frenchmen, Wilfred Monod and Lemaître, and even Barth's friends, Bultmann, Gogarten and Brunner, have here, as Winkler says, a common platform against Karl Barth and what they call his one-sided and exaggerated conception of the sovereignty of the hidden God.

As mentioned above, this is not a question of historical exegesis, but a burning and present problem of Continental theology, with immediate consequences for the Churches and for politics. Theologians and Church leaders, for various reasons, are interested in maintaining this common platform against the new theology.

3. THEOLOGY OR ACTION

Understandable opposition to this theology comes from practical theologians and Church leaders, such, for instance, as Otto Dibelius, or from Church politicians like Hirsch and Bishop Müller, who have no use for a revealed God who remains hidden, for a Christian experience which is not tangible and cannot be handled as spiritual capital nor taught as other ideals can be taught. *Ecclesiam habemus*—"We have a Church"—wrote General Superintendent Dibelius, recently deposed in the German Revolution. He believes that there exist in the experience of Christian faith certain principles which are sufficiently clear to regulate Church missions, Christian education, Christian apologetics, Church politics, and even the necessary struggle against the State. He sees in this subtle new thought either a theology which makes clear things obscure or a "theology of increasing protestation." The next lecture will show that a large group of Christians in Germany hold the same position. They take their point of departure from the material principle of the Reformation, justification by faith, using it as they understand it, as an obvious, given instrument which has been placed in their hands, a well known, clearly definable and palpable principle upon which a new Church and perhaps even a new nation may be built. You have here the opposition of a laymen's theology, of the practical faith of the plain man in the street, to a professorial theology of dogmatic subtlety and philosophical abstraction; Christian experience, as a relatively simple thing, over against theology as a product of meticulous thinking. The practical Christian abhors *"fides quaerens intellectum"* (the title of Barth's book on Anselm of Canterbury), a "faith which seeks intellectual expression," because this leads to unfruitful, theoretical discussions and to party conflict and hatred at a time when practical considerations call for unity in a Church now locked in vital struggle with the State and the World. The "German Christians," of whom we shall speak later, have openly declared war on Barthian theology in the name of a theology of life and action which is not isolated from real life. Prominent theologians like Erich Seeberg and Adolf Koeberle support this criticism by pointing out that Barth's theology is

75

RELIGION AND THE EUROPEAN MIND

"reinforcing the separation of theology from life,"
as was done by Ritschl, and that this isolation is
leading to utter paralysis of practical action.

4. BIBLE OR HISTORY

A new point is raised here against a theology of
the Word: the importance of history in the process
or fact of revelation. When Barth says that the
Gospel, as a transcendent absolute fact, cannot be
introduced as a party element into the practical
opposites of life, Erich Seeberg and the school of
Karl Holl (notably Emanuel Hirsch) hold that the
fact of incarnation means God's entrance into human
history. There is never such a thing as a "pure
theology"; theology expresses its content in terms
of a given historical period. There is no abstract
Gospel, no abstract theology, since every theology
is deeply penetrated by the interests, the practical
conflicts and aims of its own generation. God is,
therefore, not limited to His "Word," but uses
history as His vehicle and speaks to us as the
unknowable God in historic events, which claim
courageous decisions from individuals as well as
from whole nations. A theology of the Word,
therefore, is not sufficient for solving the problems
of life, but "the Word *and* history" together represent God's incessant action in the world. God's
educative influence can be found concretely in the
Church and in the creatures through whom He
speaks. "The Word would be dead if it were not
always reaching us through the events of history

and through great leaders." God is the God of history. He steers it; He uses it as His mouthpiece, as His instrument. He is concealed in its processes. He does not act upon us like an exploding shell—(an image which was used by Barth in his *Epistle to the Romans*)—a shell which only frightens us; but if He crushes us, it is for the purpose of using us as His co-operators, His organs, in which, according to Luther, God Himself is "praying, preaching, and doing good." We shall see later how this theology of history serves the "German Christians," who pretend to hear and follow God as manifest in living history as a justification for their activities. Erich Seeberg, in advocating a theology of history, goes so far as to see the real theological problem of the present time in the alternative: "Bible or History?" and asks: "Does evangelical theology need an historical and philosophical basis, or can it indeed be a theology of the Word and of the Word alone?" It becomes quite clear here *Why* Barth has had to protest against the conjunction *and*—the Word *and* history, revelation *and* reason, theology *and* philosophy, revelation *and* conscience. He sees here human elements—experience, conscience, reason, historic claims—co-ordinated with the exclusive principle of God's sovereignty in such a way as to make man God's partner, forgetful of the fact that God is his Creator and Judge. Barth goes so far in his criticism of such a theology of synthesis as to say even of Christian ethics: "A system of ethics which pretends to know and to establish the commandment of The Creator usurps the throne of God, poisoning the sources of faith. It is more devastating for Christian life than all the cinemas and dance halls put together!" His effort is to keep God's sovereignty unmixed with human elements. "God is in heaven and man on earth," he reiterates; the Gospel has nothing in common either with the open Cartesianism of the older theology or with the cryptic Cartesianism of this new immanentist theology.

5. CONCRETE OR ABSTRACT THEOLOGY

Another front is drawn up before dialectic theology by those who defend the certainty of faith against Barth's apparent refusal to define God's act and will, that is, against his conception of the hidden God, his dialectical refusal to make any concrete utterance concerning the real and lasting relationship between God and man. Reference must be made here to Karl Heim who, with Althaus and Barth, is one of the leading theologians of Europe. Heim is himself one of the most remarkable exponents of that movement which led to the revival of the Reformation. In his *magnum opus*, *Glaube und Denken*, he seeks not only to emphasize afresh the fundamental fact of the Reformation, but to justify it in the philosophical terms of our own day. He tries to orient the evangelical message in the tremendous need of the contemporary generation—a need of which Heidegger's nihilistic philosophy of fear, despair and death is the characteristic expression. Heim becomes a philosopher for the philosophers, a layman for the laymen, a plain-thinking Christian who has laid aside philosophy's language of mystery (which he himself has admirably mastered) in order "to put the essentials of the Gospel on the market of current opinions and public questions." He entirely agrees with modern philosophy that the unity of thinking and being on which idealistic philosophy was based is irreparably lost, and that we can never fall back on the egocentric philosophy of Descartes—this because we have discovered the real and enigmatic *Thou* above the *Ego*. He enters resolutely into the epistemological pessimism of "existential" philosophy by emphasizing the fact that all our explanations end in a reduction to something which we can no longer explain. All our existence is a part of a mystery which surrounds even scientific thinking, so that nothing is left to us but grace or despair. But this mystery of grace does not remain a mere nebulous question. It becomes concrete in the life of the Christian. It is made real in the manifestation of God in Christ. We cannot dispense it. It remains God's act and gift.

So far, Heim entirely approves the position of Barth, of whom he says: "He swung the tiller of theology hard so that the whole Church 'came about.' " He credits Barth with opening wide the unbridgeable crevasse between God and man, the chasm which "cannot be closed by the treacherous snow-bridges of mystical experience or by any doctrine of sanctification purporting to re-establish direct relationship with God."

But here he asks Karl Barth whether his theology of despair is a concrete reality or only "emotional thunder"; whether it is based on the practical life of faith; whether Christian theology starts with the authority of the Church, with its acts of baptism, involving certainty of faith, or—as Calvin taught— with an act of the Holy Spirit in the heart of the believer. A practical and concrete act of confession or commitment to Christ is the condition of all utterances which theology may make concerning faith in Christ. Again, a general confession of sin which is not premised on concrete living is not really a confession of sin, but a flight from it, or an empty phrase. The fear of seeming superior to God should not prevent us from listening to the concrete commandments He gives us. Otherwise we express in a negative way a feeling of superiority to God, by trying to limit His liberty of speaking to us in the way He wills. He speaks to us concretely and not as Barth's hidden God, asking obedience without telling us directly what He desires us to do.

This attack on Barthian theology, which Barth declares to be due to a misinterpretation of his thought, shows how immediate is the problem of contemporary theology in Germany. Theology there is confronted with the fundamental question of what the Gospel means, while the country is practically in the midst of a revolution requiring that practical decisions be made quickly. Theology, with its eternal problems, with its tendency to systematize and to dogmatize, with its balanced doctrines, is again being asked: What shall we do with all this? How shall we act in God's name and in obedience to His will, if this will is hidden and inexpressible in any concrete form—if the Christian in practical life is for ever suspended between the *yea* of faith and the *nay* of reflection?

This is a serious attack on the dialectical method itself, with its balance between *yea* and *nay*, its recurring crises before God, its dialectical tension between a rigid Biblical supernaturalism and a scepticism which hardly dares to act except in those rare and uncertain moments when God speaks in the personal decisions of faith. The last century was in danger of indulging uncritically in a certainty of faith and of taking God's mystery as an unveiled and accessible manifestation of an all-too-well-known God. At the present time, an important part of German theology has fallen largely into the opposite danger of indulging indefinitely in critical reflection, forgetting to make the decisions of faith naturally and so to act. This must be kept in mind if we are to understand the vigorous reaction of the "German Christians" who, in a time of epoch-making events, have not been able to wait until all theological conceptions are clarified.

Limitations of space prevent more than a mention of a remarkable book by Bonhoefer, who tries to solve the problem by making a differentiation between faith as an act and faith as being, as existence; between a static and a dynamic conception of God's revelation in Christ, both of which are conceived as constituent elements in Christian life and thinking.

This criticism of Barth's dynamic interpretation of God's revelation is widely shared by the followers of Holl, who find certainty given by God in the conscience, and by the Pietists, who by the testimony of their inner life feel assured of their faith.

6. FAITH AS CERTAINTY OR AS PARADOX

The battle is, perhaps, hottest at the point of this particular problem. Barth stands somewhat alone in his attempt to safeguard the exclusive dynamic sovereignty of God by confining its manifestation to the particular dynamic event of this or that decisive moment in the life of the Christian. He quotes the old Reformed theologians, Boehl and Kohlbruegge, as corroborating his position. It was the latter who repudiated all Christian Cartesianism or Immanentism, and once uttered deeply moving words concerning a faith based not upon sweet inner experiences or speculative or ethical certainty, but upon Christ and His Word: "If some one, after I am dead, should find my skull, it would preach to him. It would say, 'I have no eyes, yet I see Christ. I have no brain nor reason, yet I hold to Him. I have no lips, yet I kiss Him. I have no tongue, yet I praise Him. I am here in the cemetery, yet I am in Paradise.' "

All direct certainty arrived at through experience, through Christian logic, or through any static interpretation of God's manifestation, Barth compares to the manna in the desert, which the Israelites tried in vain to keep for more than one day. The manna of faith, according to him, is not a reserve fund on which we can rely and on which we may live for ever. It is given to us as food for soul and body only by a momentary and ever-renewed act of God Himself. Faith is a miracle to wonder at and not a soft cushion to sleep on. It is the mysterious and sovereign act of God opening man's heart from above, not a human *receptaculum* filled with unevaporating supernatural cognitions.

7. DENOMINATIONALISM OR PROTESTANTISM?

Another storm-centre is the question of denominationalism. The rebirth of the spirit of the Reformation leads back naturally not only to the great common principles of the Reformation, but also to the unfortunate schism and individual theological motives of the reformers. The second lecture indicated the origin of these differences, and showed also the collaboration between the two bodies which has been characteristic of the situation in recent years—at least, in the field of common practical interests. Denominationalism has little meaning in Germany to-day for the ordinary Christian consciousness. A large part of the Protestants in Germany feel themselves to be simply evangelicals. That they are members of Lutheran or Reformed Churches they regard as a minor matter. The migration of the people from place to place and their consequent attendance at various Churches, together with the striking illustration of comity in the Prussian Church Union of a hundred years ago, have had the effect on ordinary Church people of neutralizing the theological differences between the two denominations. It was part of the programme of the "German Christians" to wipe out these denominational nuances which had in times past brought so much discord into the Church, and to develop one great Evangelical German Church of a union type. But the denominational theologians were awake to this danger, and alarmed the denominational interests to such an extent that there are two or three denominational fronts, now thoroughly reinforced, in the struggle for a new Church in Germany. A new Lutheran front was formed, even before the revolution, by some exclusive Lutherans like Professor Elert in Erlangen, General Superintendent Zoellner in Westphalia, Wilhelm Stapel, editor of an influential nationalist magazine, and Professor Schomerus in Leipzig.

They have not forgotten the day of Marburg, and every attempt made in the direction of union is abhorred by this denominational group. Its members are to be found mostly in the Lutheran circles of Saxony and Bavaria. The Church union formed in Prussia in 1817, under King Frederick William, although it was a mere union of administration and not a confessional one, has been an object of constant and bitter attack. The practice of the German Evangelical Church of the Augsburg and Helvetic Confessions in Poland, and of the Church of Hessen, where Holy Communion is celebrated simultaneously under both forms, is little less than horrible to the Old Lutherans of the

Confessio Augustana invariata. The feeling of the latter is shared by those Lutherans in America who have been willing to grant their help on condition that joint communion services cease. The conception of a joint Protestant body, including Lutherans and Calvinists, is declared a typically Melanchthonian error.

It is not easy to define what theological differences separate the two great historical groups at the present day. It is no longer simply the doctrine of the Holy Communion, as in the day of Marburg. From the Lutheran side, the Reformed doctrine, especially in the form of the dialectical theology, is subjected to the criticism that it replaces the historical opposites, sin and grace, by two others, creature and God—as if every creature, as such, everything that belongs to the fallen world, were in need of reconciliation; as if "apple-trees and storks, as creatures, needed the pardon of the Gospel." The pessimism of the dialectical movement is condemned because it leaves no place for man to praise God for His creation. For the Lutherans the theology of the infinite qualitative difference between time and eternity lacks the joyous spirit of Luther's faith; Luther did not see any deep gulf between God and His creation—only that gulf between God and sinners which is definitely bridged by the Gospel. The Gospel allows us, according to Luther, to take joy in the gifts of nature, in the little flowers, and in God's kindness towards His children.

Another object of discord is the alleged legalism

in the Reformed conception of ethics. Lutheran theology accuses the Reformed Church of preaching the law—even the law of the Old Testament—to the neglect of the evangelical liberty of faith, which was Luther's great discovery. It is pointed out that the Old Testament plays a larger part in the Reformed Church—*vide* Puritanism—than in Lutheranism; and that for the latter the danger does not exist that human or Christian social programmes (as, for instance, Prohibition) might be glorified as the law or will of God. We may observe, even at this point, certain connections between the theology and the practical attitude of the German people in their politics.

This connection is still plainer in the alleged affinity of Lutheranism with monarchism, and of Calvinism with democracy. Democracy, both the word and the concept, is at present in bad repute in the German nation. In any kind of a monarchal institution the genuine Lutheran sees represented the moral values of personal responsibility. The leader feels responsible to God, who has called him to his office. He therefore represents to the world a part of God's authority, which must be obeyed. The Calvinists, on the other hand, yield to that "imaginary dream of a Christian State," where the government is vested in an anonymous collective body of elected individuals who are responsible "to law, to paragraphs and articles," and subject to the approval of an irresponsible multitude. Anything that seems akin to democratic Parliamentarianism is strongly under censure in

Germany to-day. Theology and politics are evidently not so remote from each other as they sometimes seem to Americans, whose Churches have no relationship to the State. What is still worse in the eyes of the Lutherans than the relation between Calvinism and democracy, is the alleged connection between Calvinism and capitalism. According to the well-known thesis of the great economist, Max Weber of Heidelberg, the spirit of Calvinism lends aid and comfort to the forces of capitalism.

The theological discussion of these differences has had tremendous reverberations in the events of the recent German Revolution. The psychology and philosophy of the nation is at present, of course, nationalist. In the eyes of the German people Luther is *the* reformer. He is the great *German*. At the celebration of Luther's four hundredth birthday, at Wittenberg, the German Minister of the Interior, Dr. Frick, as well as other official dignitaries, praised Luther not so much as a hero of the faith as a hero of the German nation. He praised Luther as a protagonist of the idea suggested in the thirteenth chapter of Paul's Epistle to the Romans, namely, that the State is not a mere organized society, but is essentially a people owing personal allegiance and obedience to a God-given magistrate or head. Luther, the German, is more popular to-day than Luther, the man of faith. He is held to have discovered and understood the German soul as a "Westerner" like Calvin never could: the genius of the German race is embodied in Luther and his work—Luther's reformation emerged from the depths of a believing heart, whilst the Calvinistic reformation was only the product of a thinking brain. The popular, prophetic, unscholarly message of Luther is being thrown into relief to-day against the humanistic and learned scholarship of Calvin, who was the first to bring the truth of the Reformation into a scientific theological system, the *Institutio*.

"The Lutheran reformation was God's call to the German nation." The recent German Revolution drew from this theological axiom the conclusion that the new German Evangelical Church should have a Lutheran character, that its bishop should be a Lutheran, and that a union with the Reformed Church—even the presence of the Reformed group itself—would constitute an almost intolerable foreign element in a real German Lutheran Church. The rejection of von Bodelschwingh as Reichsbishop was not wholly due to political sympathies; confessional considerations played a part also. A certain measure of collaboration between Lutheran and Reformed groups within the national Church has been achieved. The Reformed members have been given special representation in the central ecclesiastical administrative body. But, in spite of this concession, a real and lasting peace has not yet been concluded between the two parties: on the one hand there is a Church group which demands a powerful episcopal Church government, limitation of the rights of the congregation and of the synod, and a close connection and friendship with the State; on the other hand there is a small

Reformed minority, standing for a democratic Church organization and for the universal priesthood of believers over against the authority of the bishop. This struggle between the two groups will not necessarily assume the character of a Church political controversy, but it will tend to deepen the theological differences; and we need not be astonished if the future should bring us a continuation of that theological controversy of which the Colloquy of Marburg, in the year 1529, was only the beginning.

The intensification of this old controversy has evidently had some influence on the conditions of the present œcumenical movements, such as "Life and Work," and "Faith and Order." There are many German Lutherans who are suspicious of these movements as tending towards the establishment of confessional union—so vehemently abhorred—and the development of a Christian internationalism entirely different from the ideals of a strongly and consciously nationalist Church. For the American public such a close connection of theological and political considerations is hardly understandable. It is foreign to all recent American tradition. Yet it would be impossible to understand the present situation in Germany without taking into account the old relation of State and Church and the natural tendency of the German mind to base everything, even politics, on abstract and profound theoretical and theological reflection. Neither Church nor State can be rationalized for the people of Germany without an underlying metaphysics or the mysticism of a *theory* which, according to an ancient etymology, means "a vision of God."

This reawakened denominationalism tries to widen the gulf between Lutheranism and Barth, the Reformed theologian. Nationalistic German Lutherans cannot forget that Barth is a Swiss, and, as the leader of a vehement opposition to the present Church government, has been declared incapable of understanding the German and Lutheran feeling underlying the revolution in State and Church. Lutherans like Doerries and Stapel, fearing what has been called the Calvinization of Lutheranism (which from the beginning has held suspect the democratic and social implications of the Genevan faith), have issued an open warning against the "smuggling" of Reformed elements into the pure Church of Luther.

It must be said that the dialectical theology has never considered itself a denominational theology. Barth himself declares it rather to be a "bit of spice" added to every theological dish, Lutheran and Reformed.

8. BARTH AGAINST THE BARTHIANS

This picture of the present theological situation as a battlefield of contradictory tendencies would not be complete if we did not add that the occasion of all these controversies—dialectic theology—is becoming more and more a battlefield itself. Its various leaders are not in agreement with each other. An inner differentiation is growing up among them.

It must be kept in mind that this group has done more for the rebirth of the spirit of the Reformation than any other theological school for a hundred years. The whole situation on the Continent has been most promisingly transformed, largely by the searching questions of the dialectical theology, and though that theology can no longer be understood as a homogeneous unit in all things, it has even now a common denominator in its emphasis on the transcendence of God, in its Biblicism and religious pessimism, its opposition to what has been called cultural Protestantism, and its character as a theology of revelation.

But to-day Barth must feel more or less isolated when he sees his friends and former followers going their own way, and realizes that he is nearly alone with his friend, Eduard Thurneysen, in the defence of the exclusive dynamism of God's transcendence. These two friends have, therefore, ceased to contribute to *Zwischen den Zeiten*—the magazine of the movement. Barth's "Nay!" to every human attempt to build bridges between God and man, or to find a synthesis between revelation and human experience, or to allow for collaboration between the Divine and the human will, is categorical. His is an absolute theology, tolerating no relatival "ifs" or "ands." God alone: *actus purus*—free mysterious personality, above all and before all! "Thou shalt have no other gods before me!": this first commandment has been declared by Barth to be the fundamental theological axiom which can never be violated with impunity.

An absolute theology is by its nature immune
from attack, but practical necessity compels most
theologians to discover points of contact with the
life and thought of their generation: to state the
practical consequences of theology for daily life in
state, social, missionary and educational work. So,
for instance, Barth's friend, Professor Bultmann
of Marburg, tries to find a preliminary ontological
basis for the dynamic act of faith, and discovers it
in that last quality of our existence resulting from
man's being confronted with death and the nihilism
of fear and despair. Whenever this existential condition is reached, whenever man realizes the limit of
his being, he is prepared for the act of faith. Bultmann, therefore, places the study of man—the
study of the primordial data of our existence—side
by side with the theology of revelation; in other
words, he places the fact of creation beside the
fact of redemption, and falls thereby under the
condemnation of Barth's "Thou shalt have no
other gods before me."

Gogarten, taking a similar stand, criticizes the
lack of a real humanism in Karl Barth's theology.
He questions also the transcendent isolation of
God from man, and man from God. It seems to
him that the development of a new theological
doctrine of man is more needed than ever in a
time when man has lost his central place in creation.
His point of departure is, therefore, "man understood as God's creature and the object of His
redemption." To comprehend God one needs a
certain comprehension of man and vice versa. Man

must, therefore, decide about God when he is confronted with the reality and the concrete claims of his neighbour. Gogarten stresses this point so strongly that Barth asks him whether God is only another name for neighbour. If God is to be found in the facts of creation itself, in the claims laid upon us by our neighbour, Gogarten is not so remote from the position of the "German Christians," who discover God in the orders of creation and the concrete claims of history. It must have been a source of great grief to Barth that this friend joined the "German Christians." (At the moment of writing he has again left the "German Christian" movement.)

Even Emil Brunner, the most systematic thinker among the dialectic theologians, has let his former connection with Karl Barth lapse. Not only has he become a friend of the First Century Fellowship Movement, working side by side with Frank Buchman, but he has tried to find a point of contact for the theology of revelation with science and practical sociology. In both instances he parts company with Barth.[1] Instead of basing theology exclusively

[1] It was for the sake of maintaining these principles that Barth finally decided to sever his connection with the journal, *Zwischen den Zeiten*. When Gogarten had come to terms with the "German Christians"—temporarily, at least—and the anthropological tendencies of his theology became more and more pronounced, Barth saw that the old combination between a *theologia naturalis* and a theology of revelation—he calls it a "lemonade"—was again presented to the Christian world as a solution for its present troubles. Quoting the apostle John, who would not stay one hour with the gnostic, Cerinthus, he left the house which he and Thurneysen had built—and thus the famous magazine, which for so many years had

93

on the axiom of the first commandment, he calls his book *Das Gebot* und *die Ordnungen* (*The Commandment* and *the Orders*), leaving it to the Christian to find those forms of obedience to this commandment which are possible for him in the incurably sin-infected orders. Brunner bases his ethics on the will of God as visible in creation and redemption, and avoiding a legalist interpretation of the commandments of the Bible, leaves the way open for the constructive effort of the Christian conscience and the incessant corrections which God applies to that effort; and in these respects he seems to be nearer to the American mind than his friend, Barth. He admits, as did Karl Holl and Luther also, that the actions of men under God's law are *larvae Dei*, masks of God, and that man is really instrumental in effecting God's will in this world.

This short survey cannot give more than a vague impression of the fact that even dialectic theology itself is a battlefield to-day. The general point of discord lies in the various interpretations of the relation between creation and redemption. There are three interpretations. Can we discover, through Christ and in the creation, certain given creative laws which are God's orders, showing us the way towards a reconstruction of the world? Or is the creation so filled with sin that we can no longer find in it the will of the Creator? Or is the creation the point of departure for redemption and justifica-

been the vehicle of all dialectical theologians, was killed, because Barth could not tolerate the heresy of the "Barthian" Gogarten!

94

tion by faith? Whenever any principle is admitted other than that of God's revelation, Karl Barth sees the way open towards the Roman Church, with its doctrine of the *analogia entis* and the *imago Dei*, or towards the old Pelagianism and the natural theology, against which the reformers struggled with all their might.

The purpose of this Lecture has been to show that the present situation in Continental theology is controversial in every respect, and can only be understood as a huge battlefront. It has been necessary to enter into these theological controversies, because the German Revolution, at least in its ecclesiastical aspects, has become more and more a theological problem.

V

GERMAN PROTESTANTISM IN CONFLICT WITH SECULARISM[1]

CONTINENTAL Protestantism is engaged not only in theological controversy, but in a decisive battle between genuine Christianity and a religion of secularism in various forms. "Religion versus religion," or rather, "the Gospel versus religion" —such a description best expresses the true character of the present spiritual struggle. This struggle has its direct repercussions in political, social and educational activity. Nationalism and Communism could not exercise such fascination on large masses of people on the Continent, if they were not *religions*. Indeed, as was pointed out in the first chapter, they are man-made religions set against a Christian faith based on God's revelation.

New battlefronts between Christ and the world are being drawn up everywhere. They are, perhaps, nowhere so distinct as in Germany, and nowhere have the issues been worked out more elaborately

[1] In this and the next chapter, reference is made to the events of the ecclesiastical revolution in Germany, not so much from the point of view of Church politics as from the point of view of the underlying principles and leading ideas around which the struggle is raging. For a description of the current events up to January 1934, reference is made to the book of Dr. Charles Macfarland, *The New Church and the New Germany*, New York, Macmillan, 1934.

in religious programmes and theological formulae than in the astounding revolution of ideals which has taken place in the German mind.

It is obvious that the fate of the largest Protestant body on the Continent, German Protestantism, will deeply affect the religious situation everywhere. It will not be amiss for us, therefore, to try to understand the religious meaning of the German Revolution, since it will affect not only the œcumenical relations between the Churches, but the interpretation of the Gospel everywhere throughout a changing world.

We should, perhaps, have said—throughout *a world which is coming to an end*. There is to-day a widespread feeling that the present world crisis means not only a sifting process leading towards a new discrimination regarding the old values of life, but a real end, the end of a myth on which the past generations lived, the end of a culture whose living force is spent, the end of a political and social system which we had believed to be permanent. Many speak of the end of European civilization, or even of its suicide, of the end of capitalism and the *bourgeoisie*, of the end of liberalism and democracy, of the end of organized religion.

Christianity has never been afraid of the end. In its eschatological message it has always announced the end of the world in which we live. The crisis, of which the Gospel speaks, is the judgment of God making way for His Kingdom.

But the new secular eschatologies of Nationalism,

Fascism and Communism do not announce the Kingdom of God; they preach other values and ideals. What are these values and ideals and how do they affect the religious life of the Continent?

We shall not enter here into political considerations, but shall confine ourselves to an understanding of the revolution in its psychological, social and religious aspects. We shall examine the new ideals and life forces which have furnished the dynamic impulse for the fundamental change in the political, social and religious life of Central Europe, especially of Germany. This is all the more necessary since neither in France nor in Germany would great political movements have broken forth without great underlying ideas, without a philosophy or a religious creed.

I. A NEW MYTH

In the National Socialist revolution a new myth has been materializing, the myth of race, the mysticism and religion of "blood" and "nation." This mysticism of blood tends to replace the mysticism of the absolute spirit and of universal human society. Humanity, an international peaceful organization of the whole world, a world Church, an idealized scientific conception of the universe —these appear to the present generation mere abstractions. The concrete reality of life is not found in the "vague" ideals of a universal humanitarianism or of Christianity, but in the red-blooded entity of the race, in the mystery of the blood which contains God's creative mystery itself. The Bible of this new myth is Alfred Rosenberg's book, *The Myth of the Twentieth Century*, which is to-day one of the most widely read books in Germany. Rosenberg is the editor of the *Voelkische Beobachter* and head of the National Socialist cultural propaganda service. The biological fact of the blood as the constituent element of a race becomes, in his cultural philosophy, a religious or metaphysical principle. Blood existed before culture or religious and political systems came into being. It is a primordial datum, a God-given law which must be obeyed. A hierarchy of mysterious values dominates God's creation. God is not on the side of democracy. In His world there is good blood filled with creative forces and bad blood tainted with vile instincts. He created superior and lower races, and it is His will that the best blood shall reign, that is, the Nordic, the Germanic race. Rosenberg declares that in this revolution the German has become conscious of inner racial values. These higher values of the race are not simply and automatically a product of evolution. They are the prize of heroic effort, of incessant fighting for manly virtues.

A new life-ideal is seen arising here. Old Nordic tales and myths support it. It is not the Christian ideal of love and compassion, which is alleged merely to have brought weak peoples and individuals under the control of mighty and more astute powers. It is the ideal of honour, which has a much stronger educational appeal than the emasculating ideal of humility and charity. The old Viking, the German knight, the Prussian officer, the Baltic baron, the German soldier and farmer are authentic exemplars of this new ideal of a heroic and manly life. The new slogan is, therefore, "With sword and plough for honour and liberty!" Rosenberg himself said to the writer, a few weeks ago, that Christian love and the protection of the weak and the sick are bad selective principles. The Christian doctrine of love, he said, is a way to slavery rather than to liberty. He claimed to find ample proof in history for his belief that a society or a nation can never really be built upon a religion of love, since this soon degenerates into a religion of exploiting the weak.

From this racial standpoint, the Jews are not only a foreign element, an inferior race, but a "dangerous poison" menacing the purity of the Germanic blood. We need not describe here the biological theory of anti-Semitism. Suffice it to say that Jewish blood is made responsible not only for the parasitism of the Jewish people, the acquisitiveness of the Jewish nature, and the consequent exploitation and unemployment of the German people, but also for the disintegrating and analytical tendency in modern art and literature, and the negative and destructive qualities embodied in Bolshevism and atheism. The present harshness in the application of the Aryan paragraph is, therefore, "the legitimate defence of the German genius against the Jewish demon as represented in Shakespeare's immortal Shylock."

The State of Adolf Hitler is doing away with this Semitic "nuisance" by establishing a nation of pure Aryan blood. The State is no longer a contract between the people and its rulers, as Rousseau understood it, nor an abstract entity, as in the philosophy of Hegel. It is the nation, the whole nation itself, and the "totalitarian" expression of all its functions.

All these elements are characteristic features of the new conception of the world, the new philosophy which has inaugurated a revolution in ideals and religion, parallel to the political revolution. The era of liberalism, with its ideals of personal liberty, freedom of teaching, liberty of migration and commerce, its parliamentarianism and socialism, equality of the sexes, emancipation of women and equality of men, has gone. Authority, civic solidarity, discipline, self-sufficiency, race consciousness, polarity of the sexes, honour, heroism, willpower: these new ideals are coming to the fore. The philosophy of the Nazi movement is no form of idealism or humanism.[1] It will have none of their insoluble problems, general principles, systems and programmes; it abhors the rule of abstract theory, which always ends in illusion. The revolution means the end of such "humanistic hallucinations." Man is confronted with reality itself and must lose no time in an impossible attempt to solve abstract problems. We see in this new attitude a parallel to similar tendencies in modern

[1] Forsthoff, *Das Ende der Humanistischen Illusion* (Berlin, 1933, Furche Verlag).

German philosophy, especially in Heidegger and Grisebach, who have turned away from a philosophy of mere consciousness towards an ontological or "existential" philosophy. They are more interested in the problem of existence than in questions of thinking. They proclaim the priority of being, whereas their predecessors held to the priority of thought. This transformation of a philosophy of cognition into a philosophy of existence—and its practical parallel in political action—is one of the most typical of the new attitudes of the European mind. Descartes' axiom, *cogito, ergo sum,* has run its course. It is now turned round: *Sum, ergo cogito.* Existence has less to do with thinking than with acting, that is, with responsible decisions by responsible personalities. This leads again to an enthronement of power, to the myth of violence and heroic effort. The French socialist, Georges Sorel, who has been advocating a social revolution not by mass movement, but by the usurpation of power by a ruthless minority, has acquired a new popularity. Many people, including certain German bishops who would not have dreamed of accepting his ideas a few decades ago, now follow him. It is evident that in the German Revolution we are not only confronted with political passions, with revolutionary action, with adventurous attempts to gain power, but with a new mentality, a new conception of life and its values, a new philosophy of the State, a new religious myth of the revolution.

What does all this mean for the Christian religion,

for the Church of Christ? An entirely new religious situation has arisen within a very short time. We are dealing not only with controversies between theological groups and ecclesiastical parties within the Church, but with new myths and religions or, at least, such new interpretations of the Gospel that we are forced to ask: Is this still the genuine Gospel of Jesus Christ, the Gospel rediscovered by the Reformation—or is it a misrepresented, diluted or polluted Gospel of a Christianity trying to justify its worldly aims through an allegedly Divine message, and blending it with mystical and mythical elements which have nothing to do with the Gospel of Christ?

2. NEW RELIGIONS

(a) We need not lose much time in describing the decidedly anti-Christian paganism represented in the *Tannenbergbund* or the artificial religion created by the wife of General Ludendorff, the right-hand man of Hindenburg during the war! Gogarten is doubtless right when he asks us not to pay too much attention to such "man-made religions."

(b) Much more serious, because based on deep scientific studies of comparative religion, are the attempts to find in all Aryan religion, from India to the northern countries, a common original religion of the Light God (the Sun), which is worshipped as the Son of God. This is a religion of Light, regarded as wandering through the months of the year, ever struggling with darkness;

killed in the winter; born again in the spring, and adored as the symbol of creative life. A new syncretism is rising here in the synthesis of the myths of Indian and Persian light gods and goddesses, of the religion of Mithras and of the eternal drama of the birth and death of light.

The God who is acting in this eternal drama is "the Great Spirit" behind the cosmic events, beyond Space and Time, the origin of all things who reveals Himself in the cosmic laws. The cosmic year is the revelation of God through His Son, who, however, is not considered as a Sun God, the sun being not more than His manifestation. Man's life is repeating this cosmic law, it is "God's year."

Hermann Wirth[1] finds the traces of this original religion in old cult symbols which he discovers again in the symbolism of the Christian religion. Christ Himself is of Aryan extraction and preached Himself the universal religion of Light by which man is redeeming himself from all the powers of darkness. In the actual German Revolution and its new religious revelation an old immanent memory of this original light-religion is reawakening, the old heritage of the blood is breaking forth.

Such ideas are not entirely new. Arthur Drews and the "free thinkers" have moved in this direction for many years. What *is* new is that these ideas are becoming the nucleus of a new positive religion, of a new Church competing with the Christian Church and claiming recognition by the new State.

(*c*) In the widely read books of Ernest Berg-

[1] *Aufgang der Menschheit*, Jena, 1928.

mann[1] and Alfred Rosenberg[2] a serious attempt
is made to show that the old northern religion,
transformed into a modern mysticism, is the sole
religion really congenial to the Germanic race.

It alone can unify the German people in one
national Church by glorifying the best mythical
elements and the most heroic ideals in the German
race. Bergmann criticizes the Christian Church,
saying that it cannot fulfil this task. He makes
Lutheranism responsible for the loss of the soul
of the German people and for the defection of the
masses from the Church. Calvinism is likewise
condemned, and, as an example of its destructive-
ness he points to Holland, where the *"furor Cal-
vinicus"* is held to have driven the people out of
the Church. The German people need a new
reformation, a new God, a new religious and moral
ideal, a German faith, and a German national
Church. The old Jewish Jahveh is a foreign God,
"quite as alien to the best of the northern race
as is the transcendent God of Barthian theology,
who annihilates the God in man, making man
merely an empty vessel, and destroying the identity
of God and man." The Reformation was, therefore, wrong in keeping the Old Testament in the
Bible and putting it into the hands of the people.
Bergmann, as well as Rosenberg, would abolish it
as an authoritative religious text. They even accuse
the apostle Paul of having adulterated the original

[1] Ernest Bergmann, *Die Deutsche Nationalkirche*, Breslau, Hirth.
[2] Alfred Rosenberg, *Der Mythos des Zwanzigsten Jahrhunderts*,
Munich, Hoheneichen Verlag.

Gospel of Jesus with Jewish elements. They quote, of course, Marcion, one of the "heretics" of the second century, approving his anti-Paulinism, his anti-Jewish attitude, and his opposition to the tyrant-God of the Old Testament who, as a bad "demiurge," an evil creative spirit, is not to be identified with the supreme, mysterious and remote Divinity. Rosenberg, who commands considerable influence through his paper, is popularizing the views of a great German scholar of the preceding century, Lagarde. The latter, in vehement attacks against the official Church, made Paul and his Semitism responsible for the failure of the Gospel in the Germanic world. Lagarde is considered to-day one of the greatest Germans, because he anticipated a truly national religion in contrast to a vague and colourless world religion. The unity of the German nation was for Lagarde of such importance that he felt that Catholicism, Protestantism, Judaism and Naturalism should and would disappear before the new national religion, as night lamps dimmed in the light of the rising sun. Rosenberg, like Lagarde, would, therefore, replace the Old Testament with a collection of Nordic tales, and would cleanse the Bible of all magical and Jewish elements, and all ideals of submission and servitude, such as are proclaimed in the myth of the Servant of God in Isaiah, the myth of the lamb of God which is slaughtered defenceless, and the myth of the Cross, which reminds the people of the failure of a heroic effort and a useless humility. In his eyes this ideal of weakness and submission has been an instrument in the hand of Rome to emasculate the German soul.

God, according to Bergmann, must be sought in the soul of the race, not in the Bible. God is a psychic content in man—not a theological, but a natural, immanent God. The German God is the friend-God, not the Jewish tyrant-God. He is the force-God, the soul-God, who is leading humanity not downward to its end, into an abyss of despair, condemnation and utter annihilation, but upward towards a higher life and more heroic ideals. "Nothing is more urgent for us Germans than to extinguish in our Nordic hearts all this appalling remembrance of a southern Christ killed cruelly on the Cross."

Rosenberg finds this psychological conception of God in the mediaeval mystic Eckhart. The German mysticism of the thirteenth century becomes the model for the new German religion. For Eckhart God is in the soul. He is "the spark" in the soul which Rosenberg interprets as the symbol of those metaphysical entities of honour and freedom which are the "interior castles" from which peace, will and reason attack the outward world. The sin of Protestantism is to have forgotten this mystical message and to have replaced it with the doctrine of the Semitic Jahveh and the "Etruscan Pope of Rome." The old Nordic Edda, the Germanic tragedy of the end of the gods in a general cataclysm, and the rebirth of new gods, was understood and rediscovered in his own soul by *Meister* Eckhart, who is, therefore, the first modern representative of the reborn German man. God, according to him, belongs so ultimately to the soul that He cannot live without man. The soul is, therefore, more than the universe, is greater than God, and in its isolation, "in its fierce independence and solitude," it enjoys a sovereignty which is really divine. The free, noble soul—neither the Church nor the Pope—is the true vicar and incarnation of God. In the freedom of the soul God and nature find a mystical union; man is in harmony with himself and, as such, quite independent of the Church or any supernatural grace. So Meister Eckhart is proclaimed by Rosenberg as the creator of the new Germanic religion, with its ideal of liberty, immanent creative power, restless action. He is the prototype of Goethe, the greatest modern German, who stood for the same ideals. "Let us therefore believe in ourselves and work out our own salvation and redemption," says Bergmann, "in a new German National Church—a Church which shall no longer teach us weak submission and patient endurance, but action, faith in ourselves and the will to achieve social justice."[1]

"We are no more Christians in the traditional sense," because Christianity meant the victory of a God with an exclusively masculine character, while humanity has to go back to the "Mother-

---

[1] Bergmann has suggested the following confession of faith (*Die Deutsche Nationalkirche*, 1933): "I believe in the God of the German religion who is at work in nature, in the lofty human spirit, and in the strength of his people. I believe in the helper, Christ, who is struggling for the noble human soul. I believe in Germany, the land of culture for a new humanity."

Spirit," opposed to the anthropomorphic Spirit-God. The traditional belief in a Man-God must be replaced by the belief in "Mother Nature," the "Great Mother." "God is dead," as Nietzsche said, namely the manly Creator-God. The idea of God must have a bi-sexual character. We meet here the tension between a philosophy of Life and a philosophy of the Spirit, a new life-religion preached many years ago by George and Klages.

Man can redeem himself. "Have faith in the lofty human spirit" is the first commandment of this religion. The spirit of man is the true Christ and in fact, "man is truly and really God Himself." Grace means the will to become Divine, and the fundamental ethical principle is to make the Divine incandescent in yourself, to enter into the process of deification.

The religion of Germany must become this natural religion, this religion of the human spirit which has to take the place of the traditional *"dementia christiana"* with its formulae of Sin, Judgment, Grace, Redemption.

These tendencies form the left wing of a natural and nationalist religion, attacking the former shallow materialism, atheism and scepticism quite as vehemently as they do traditional Christianity which, as a supernatural religion, is not considered as a suitable faith for the German people. This wing is represented not merely by isolated individual writers, such as Bergmann, Rosenberg, Reventlow, Niedlich, Blueher, Krieck, Gerstenbauer, Anderson, but also by organized groups which are gathering members into growing fellowships such as the *Deutschglaeubige Gemeinschaft, Die Nordische Religioese Arbeitsgemeinschaft, Adler und Falke, Rig, Bund der Freireligioesen Gemeinden, Freundeskreis der Kommenden Gemeinde, Gemeinschaft Deutscher Erkenntnis,* claiming thousands of members. These various groups have formed recently an "Association of German Faith," confessing an open paganism and exerting considerable missionary influence. Professor Hauer has become the president of this association, including various tendencies, the common denominator of which may be found in an anti-Christian, anti-dogmatic, pantheistic mysticism, in the belief in the immanent Divine faculties of the human soul.

This man-made religion has already gained such influence that Dr. von Bodelschwingh raised his warning voice. The German people have to face the question whether they shall believe in Siegfried or in Christ. The political programme is to ask for nothing less than recognition by the State as a "Third Confession,"[1] or denomination, on a par with the Catholic and Evangelical Churches, with equal rights in universities, schools, parishes, missionary activity and the Press.

Between this left wing of the present-day religious forces in Germany and the more traditional forms of Christianity there stands an important body, the "German Christians," which, from the angle of Church politics, must be regarded as the key group in the present situation.

[1] See the symposium, *Die dritte Konfession,* Berlin, 1934.

3. THE "FAITH MOVEMENT" OF THE GERMAN CHRISTIANS

The fellowship of the "German Christians" is not a homogeneous group. The common denominator of its various elements is the synthesis which they believe they have established between faith in the new racial and national ideals and the traditional belief in Christ. They have in common the conviction that "the people and religion belong together," that the Church cannot remain indifferent to the great national upheaval, that the new State and its leader, Adolf Hitler, are instruments in the political, moral and religious rebirth of the whole nation. They call themselves a "faith movement" because they believe in the religious significance of the race as God-given, and in the Gospel as the deepest constructive character-building power in a nation. The differences between the various groups within the party are concerned, for the most part, with the question of the relative emphasis to be laid on the rôle of nationalism. "We see in our time," said Bishop Rentdorff of Mecklenburg (since resigned from office), "two mighty currents, the roar of which stirs our hearts. We know that they come from the same eternal source. We pray that these two distinct rivers may flow together into one single, powerful stream. The two currents are faith and nationality." In the opinion of the spiritual and political leaders, the appointed time for the Church is now at hand. The theologians

III

of the group, notably Professor Hirsch,[1] have made a considerable effort to justify the emotional nationalist tendencies of the day from the view-point of Christian theology—at least from the view-point of a Christian philosophy of history. History is the meeting-place of God and man. God can be found only in that mixture of natural life and spiritual, moral and religious forces which is the historical process. God is not found in abstract, idealistic existence, but in the concrete, historical events with which He confronts our conscience. We must choose between the various concrete possibilities of our destiny. It would be unchristian to try to escape from such practical decisions as are demanded of a people in a time of national rebirth. God's hidden will is manifest in the great historical events of our time. These are the *larvae Dei*, God's masks, behind which our conscience may, if it will, recognize His eternal, creative power.

A new accent is here given to the concept of creation in contrast to that of redemption. God gave to His creation certain fundamental laws or orders which are still discoverable. Though obscured by sin, the "orders" of creation—sex, family, property, marriage, State and nature—are the result of God's will; they represent the natural law which He has given to us for protection against the disintegrating influence of the forces of evil. Without this protection of natural law we should be led into chaos and destruction. God has, in

[1] Hirsch, *Das kirchliche Wollen der deutschen Christen*, Berlin, Max Gravemeyer, 1933.

particular, instituted the State (*vide* Romans xiii). Those who oppose the State oppose God Himself. The State, as Luther said, is God's servant, designed to oppose the reign of Satan. An extraordinary effort is being made to find, in a kind of State-theology, or political ethics, a theological basis for the present State. Hirsch, Gogarten,[1] Stapel,[2] Wagner, Wienecke, Hossenfelder,[3] Dingraeve, Bogner, Kolbenheyer and many other writers, are all trying to establish religious principles for political action, as are likewise the influential magazines, *Die Tat* and *Deutsches Volkstum*. Politics and religion are converging in theory as well as in practice. Hirsch goes so far as to say that the establishment of a political ethics is the real theological need of our time. It again becomes clear that the nature of Protestantism is more nearly akin to a national state than is Roman Catholicism with its international or super-national character. In the theology of nationalism, as proclaimed by William Stapel, philosophy, theology, politics and the Bible are blended in a way which constitutes a serious critical problem for any Christian theologian. For Stapel, "Christ and Caesar belong together." The future *Kaiser* (Caesar) of a new Christian *Reich* under German hegemony will be the protector of Europe and of the Church, a true servant of Christ. As a postulate of Christian theology, therefore, a new Teutonic Emperor is

[1] F. Gogarten, *Politische Ethik*, Jena, Diedrichs.
[2] W. Stapel, *Der Christliche Staatsman*, Hamburg, Hanseatische Verlaganstalt. [3] J. Hossenfelder, *Unser Kampf*.

demanded. "The Cross and the Swastika do not exclude each other." On the contrary, Reichsbishop Müller sincerely believes that the "German Christians" take Christ seriously, as a master to whom they owe allegiance and fidelity. He professes to "know no higher task than to bring the German people under the reign and rule of Christ." It is certain that many "German Christians" desire nothing more than to serve Christ in the midst of the new nation whose moral and political ideals they share. The question, however, that we must put to them is whether they have given sufficient theological thought to their new Christology, which appears to be based upon a syncretistic conception of a Christ who, as in the old epic,[1] *Der Heliand*, is pictured as a generous and noble duke, riding at the head of his clan.

To Bishop Hossenfelder, former leader of the "German Christians," Christ is an heroic fighter, a helper and conqueror, rather than the mediator between God and man. "Be pious; be German," says Hossenfelder, "and the living God will give you your daily bread." Christ is the teacher of truth and strength rather than the redeemer from sin and guilt. The "Faith Movement" of the "German Christians" acknowledges Christ as the sole master and sees in His person and life "the true essential Gospel." His Divine message is found not only in the Bible, but in the depths of the human

[1] *Vide* Dr. Otto Borchert, *Der Goldgrund des Lebensbildes Jesu* or the English edition, *The Original Jesus*, pp. 102–106. Lutterworth Press, London.

soul and in historic events as well. Christians, therefore, must listen not only to the Bible, but to the
Spirit also—and to the men in whom the Spirit
is alive. For the latter they have not far to seek
since, by God's grace, a new sun is rising for the
German nation in the person of Adolf Hitler.
A "German Christian" finds it intolerable to conceive of Jesus as a Jew. To the extreme anti-Semites,
Christ, as described by Herr Jaeger (member of
the Government and High Commissioner of State
for the Church) is a fair, blue-eyed, slender and
dolichocephalic Aryan, who signifies "the flaming
up of the best in the northern race in the midst of
a disintegrating world."

It is impossible for the Church to ignore either
the national Christianity of the "German Christians" or the "Christian" or pagan nationalism
of the extreme wings. Both groups confront the
Church squarely not only with religious ideas, but
with a determined will to build a new Church on
the basis of these ideas and to use political means
to gain control of all important posts in such a
Church.

The issue means an open fight—and such a fight
is in full swing at the present moment. The spiritual
and theological battlelines of this struggle are more
significant than its day-by-day shifting events.
Nevertheless, our story would be incomplete without
at least, a brief survey of recent developments.[1]

[1] See Heinrich Weinel, *Die deutsche evangelische Kirche*, Gotha
Klotz, 1933.

4. REVOLUTION AND CHURCH POLITICS

When Adolf Hitler, on March 11, 1933, proclaimed the German Revolution, he promised to respect the existing treaties and rights of the Churches and to secure for them their proper influence in school and education. He recognized the value of their work and expected that they, on their part, would appreciate what the State was doing for the rebirth of the nation.

Soon thereafter the "German Christians" demanded the formation of a Reichskirche which should be "in tune" with the totalitarian State. Thereupon the Lutheran and Reformed denominational groups immediately presented *their* views concerning the constitution of the proposed Church —with special reference to the appointment of bishops. A committee of three, to which, later, Chaplain Müller, a friend of Hitler, was added, drew up a consitution, and proposed Pastor von Bodelschwingh as candidate for Reichsbishop. The "German Christians," who wanted Müller elected, vehemently opposed von Bodelschwingh's candidature. The latter, realizing that his nomination lacked the necessary support, withdrew.

Dr. von Bodelschwingh is a great Christian soul, a leader in practical charitable work, a man universally beloved by the Christian people of Germany. But the political wisdom of nominating him for Reichsbishop before the functions of that office had been clearly defined or any agreement reached with the State, may be questioned.

The Church elections of July 23rd were a sweeping victory for the " German Christians." Despite violent opposition from the ecclesiastical minority group, the "Church and Gospel" (*Evangelium und Kirche*), Chaplain Müller was elected bishop of the Prussian Church. The minority group, protesting against the methods used by the "German Christian" majority and the application of the Aryan paragraph to the Church, withdrew from the Prussian Synod. The National Synod, which met on September 27, 1933, elected Bishop Müller Reichsbishop, adopted a constitution and appointed an "ecclesiastical ministry" to replace the provisional Church council.

The new Reichsbishop at once issued a proclamation stating that under the new régime the confessional heritage of the various church denominations would be safeguarded, and that the new united Church would stand firmly on the material principle of the Reformation, "justification by faith" alone. "Equality before God, however, does not include inequality before men," he said in justification of the Aryan paragraph, which excludes pastors of Jewish extraction from the ministry. "The German Evangelical Church, though not to be considered a 'State Church,' assumes full responsibility towards the State and is willing to collaborate in the building up of a new nation." . . . "The State remains State and the Church remains Church"—with her own independent religious and missionary functions.

Notwithstanding this pledge, an effort was soon

made to assimilate the Christian Youth Movement into the National Youth Movement, under Baldur von Shirach. Dr. Stange, Director of the "Christian Youth," protesting the loyalty of his organization to the national ideals, succeeded for a time in maintaining relative independence for the group. He was obliged, however, in the end to yield, and the "Christian Youth" was amalgamated with the "Hitler Youth." Moreover, an agreement has been reached between the Church government and the foreign missions societies, in accordance with which these societies, though permitted to maintain a certain independence, are closely affiliated with the Church, especially in financial matters. A similar co-ordination has been effected in the case of home missions.

The Reichsbishop finally announced that party conflicts within the Church had come to an end; that now the struggle for the soul of the people had begun, a struggle in the nature of a new and organized "people's mission." Subsequent events, however, do not bear out this assertion. On the contrary, the strife seems just to be beginning!

5. THE STRUGGLE FOR AN EVANGELICAL CHURCH

An open Church revolution broke out when, at a mass-meeting of the "German Christians" in Berlin, November 13th, the radical forces under the leadership of Pastor Krause made a direct attack on the historic Christian faith. No action was taken at the time by the Church leaders present, but shortly afterwards a group of 2,000 pastors issued a joint protest. The "Pastors' Emergency League" was formed which, within a very short time, numbered 10,000 adherents from among the Protestant ministers in Germany and the pressure brought to bear on the Reichsbishop by this organization was so strong that he was forced to annul certain Church laws—among them the Aryan paragraph. Hossenfelder resigned as Bishop of Brandenburg, and the Reichsbishop himself desisted, for the time being, from open encouragement of the "German Christians"—though, at the same time, he prohibited all political activity on the part of the protesting pastors.

But the revolt of the evangelicals was not thus easily and quickly to be put down. Southern Protestant Germany was unanimous in its opposition to the ecclesiastical policy of the Church government. Many sincere Christians who had joined the "German Christians" in the hope of a great Christian rebirth of the nation withdrew from membership; among these were Professors Schumann, Gogarten and Fezer, Bishop Schoeffel and several other influential leaders. A declaration issued by the Pastors' Emergency League, protesting against the whole policy of oppression and the attack on the Bible and the creed made by the "German Christians," was read from the pulpits. Some bishops, especially those in Southern Germany, refused to obey the authority of the Reichsbishop, and in the Rhineland synods and groups of pastors refused to accept his orders, quoting from the Bible

(Acts v. 29): "We ought to obey God rather than men."

The ecclesiastical ministry was dissolved and the "Faith Movement of the German Christians" seemed to be in process of disintegration, while the Pastors' Emergency League, under the able leadership of Pastor Niemöller of Dahlem, a suburb of Berlin, becoming increasingly outspoken in its opposition to the arbitrary measures of Church government, assumed an increasing significance in the fight for evangelical liberty. Much of their influence within the Church was lost, however, when the bishops, after a mysterious conference with Hitler, who up to that time had maintained a more or less neutral attitude, agreed to end their opposition to the Reichsbishop and to invite their ministers to collaborate faithfully with the Church government. It is not quite clear just what influences brought about this astounding decision on the part of the bishops: perhaps it was due to the persuasive powers of Hitler; possibly to a warning that the State would withdraw its financial support of the Churches or that the Secret State Police would be employed against offenders.

In spite of this submission of the bishops, however, the Church revolution is still going on. Since January 24th the Reichsbishop has taken disciplinary action against more than two hundred pastors, but the League is fighting on, undismayed. Its reaction to these measures of force and repression —a clear violation of the fundamental laws of the Church—is a reiterated declaration concerning the nature of the Gospel and the Church. Protesting congregations and "free" synods, as for instance in Barmen, Dortmund and Southern Germany, have declared the "German Christians" heretics and the Church government unbiblical. They have exhorted fellow-Christians to disobey the Church government in the name of true obedience to God.

The significance of this Church revolution lies in the fact that it is less concerned with problems of politics and Church polity than with problems of faith. Out of it is emerging an heroic trust in the truth of the Gospel, a brave reliance upon the validity of the theological doctrines of the Reformation. Once again the old phrases, *soli Deo gloria* and *sola fide*, have become battle-cries in a struggle for those fundamental religious and theological principles which are inseparable from any truly evangelical Church. We may analyse the situation under the following aspects:

(a) *The Fight for the Purity of the Gospel*

An evangelical group within the Church is fighting for the heritage of the Reformation against modern religious paganism and against the pollution of the evangelical doctrine by such secular and political interests as are described in the fourth chapter. Numerous bodies—provincial synods, pastoral assemblies, theological faculties—and individual Church leaders are participating in these efforts. We may classify them under three headings:

First, there are the old confessional groups of the Lutheran and Reformed Church parties, who are rising to defend the evangelical tradition. The Lutherans are endeavouring to bring about the foundation of the new Church on a Lutheran basis —specifically, on the declaration of faith as contained in the Augsburg Confession of 1530 and in Luther's Catechism. Their initiative has stimulated similar efforts on the part of the Reformed groups, who regard the Heidelberg Catechism as the valid confession of faith. Both groups favour a reorganization of the Church on a new national basis, but see in the old historic confessions of faith and in the emphasis upon confessional declarations the best guarantee against paganism, as well as against a vaguely generalized Christianity.

A second group, *die Jung-Reformatorische Bewegung* (the Young Reformation Movement), likewise stands for the historic continuity of the Church of the Reformation and for the maintenance of its distinctive confessional features. Among its members are such leaders as Dr. Kuenneth of Berlin, Professor Schreiner of Rostock, Dr. Hans Lilje, Secretary of the Christian Student Movement, Professor Brunstaed, Dr. Knak, Professor Karl Heim in Tübingen, The Rev. Dr. Jacobi, Professor Lütgert, Dr. Von Tiling and Professor Staehelin. The Young Reformation Movement opposes any attempt to find the solution of the present Church problems in a confessional union or fusion.[1] They object particularly to the United Prussian Church, although the nature of this union is administrative rather than con-

[1] *Die Nation vor Gott*, Walter Kuenneth and Helmut Schreiner, Wichern, Berlin, 1933.

fessional. They demand a reconstruction of the German Church along lines that are free of all political considerations. The new Church, they hold, must grow out of the old, the true character of which they find expressed in its confession of faith and in Church discipline. They are taking an active part in the struggle against modern heresies, such as the nationalist or racial religion of the *Tannenbergbund*, and the Nordic or Aryan paganism as set forth in the writings of Herrmann Wirth, Ernest Bergmann, Alfred Rosenberg, Hauer and others. This battle must be waged, they assert, by a Church which, alive as never before to the social and psychological distress of the masses and sharing their despair and economic destiny, holds in loyalty and love to a State which judges, governs and defends itself according to the law of God.

A third group in this struggle for the purity of the Gospel is represented by Karl Barth and his intransigent friends of the Reformed Confession, supported in some measure by the Pastors' Emergency League. Barth himself has published a brochure entitled *Theologische Existenz heute* (*Theological Existence To-day*), in which he attacks with unusual spiritual independence and moral courage every group within the Church which is trying to base the life of the Church on anything else than the Gospel. Because the souls of Christians have become confused in the struggle of Church politics, he stresses with exceptional vigour and earnestness the necessity for clear theological thinking. Against any attempt to discover God in a given order of creation or in an historical event of modern times, he emphasizes the old evangelical truth: "God can be found nowhere save in His Word. This Word is Jesus Christ. Christ can be found only in the Bible of the Old and New Testaments. The heart of the Church must not be divided between her political or ecclesiastical interests and the cause of the Gospel. *The Gospel alone is her care and great concern.*" Barth accuses the Church of having been "unfaithful to herself." Even the Young Reformation Movement, he charges, has stained its evangelical faith by undue interest in Church politics, citing in particular their participation in the quarrel about the Reichsbishop candidature. Such action seems to him a fatal co-ordination of the Church with the programme of the State. The new Church, he alleges, has confounded the Gospel with politics. It is his fervent hope that the new reformation may be not simply a harmonization of State and Church, but a genuine rebirth of the Evangelical Church through the power of the Word of God. He preaches repentance, therefore, and a new submission to the one head of the Church, Jesus Christ. The Church can recognize no master other than Him.

Barth does not find the purity of evangelical doctrine sufficiently safeguarded in the position of the Young Reformation Movement. In their political anti-liberalism and their interest in a theological synthesis between creation and redemption, nature and grace, nation and Gospel, he sees again the fatal theology of the "both-and," the dangerous modern syncretism between the Divine and the human. To meet this danger theological vigilance is called for, and resistance to every attempt to settle the present difficulties in the light of practical considerations of Church politics. Before the Church can deal with questions of organization and structure, theological concepts must be clarified. The theologian, Barth maintains, should continue his watch like "a lonely bird on the rooftop which under wide, free sky still rests secure on earth."

Under the courageous leadership of this outstanding theologian of the Reformed opposition, the Reformed group, though numerically weak, by virtue of its clear thinking has come to the front. He has elaborated a confession of faith, which in January 1934 was adopted by a "free" Reformed Synod in Barmen.[1] It is concerned, almost exclusively, with fundamental theological questions; even problems of Church organization are considered as questions of faith and theology. Barth has evidently forged the weapons for the ecclesiastical revolt which is now raging throughout all Germany. It is an opposition to the *theologia naturalis*; to the authority of men and parties within the Church; to mere denominational interests; to revelation in creation and history; to the value of a latitudinarian piety; to the exclusion of the Old Testament; to any moralistic or legalistic interpretation of God's sovereign grace; all these tenets have been adopted by many large free synods and

[1] See Appendix III.

125

pastoral assemblies. His positive interpretation of the message of the Church and the nature of the Gospel has become, so to speak, the unofficial creed of numerous free groups and fraternities within the Church.

The Reformed position has thus become the invincible bulwark of the opposition, the Rhineland its real fortress. While in the rest of Germany the Pastors' Emergency League is battling to defend the liberty and rights of the Evangelical Church, the "Fraternities" of ministers in the Rhineland and some independent congregations are rapidly becoming the living mother cells of a new Church, based on the great, rediscovered truths of the Reformation—the "Word of God" and "justification by faith." A convincing rebirth of the spirit of the Reformation becomes increasingly manifest, a growing insight into the true nature of the Church as called into life by the Spirit of Christ, subject to no other master.

The National Socialist revolution, in so far as it has penetrated the Church, has led to the attempt to interpret the Gospel in terms of national ideals, to co-ordinate the Christian Church to the national state and to identify the National Social revolution with a rebirth of the truly Christian spirit in the German race. This interpretation has found its classical expression in the theses of Rengsdorf.[1] In refuting the nationalist and racial creed of a new Germanist Christianity the Reformed and evangelical opposition in the Rhineland has made it

[1] See Appendix II.

indubitably clear that the actual struggle in the Church is of a theological nature.[1] In these theses and antitheses *Reformation stands against Revolution,* a Biblical Christianity against a secularized Christian ideal. Any co-ordination between the Gospel and the racial ideal is most vigorously opposed. The two can never be equal in authority, because revelation is not found in nature, nor in the voice of conscience, nor in historic events, but exclusively in the Bible of both Old and New Testaments. The reality of history or nature can never be compared with the reality of revelation in Christ. The Church, as a Divine institution, can never be assimilated into the national state, which is not a *datum* of the original creation, but an order for the maintenance of a minimum of justice in a fallen world.

The Word of God is the Church's one foundation. Where it is replaced by or co-ordinated with a political confession—as, for instance, in the declaration of Loerzer, a leader of the German Christians, that "Gospel and National Socialism are the two pillars of the German Church"—the very nature of the Church is falsified. Where National Socialism is considered the fulfilment of the Reformation, the essential message and nature of the latter fails to be comprehended. The fundamental problem of the Church revolution is to interpret aright the meaning of the Reformation. The struggle, therefore, can no longer be regarded as an ex-

[1] See *Artgemaesses Christentum oder Schriftgemaesser Christusglaube,* Joachim Beckmann, Essen, 1933.

clusively German affair, but becomes a matter
affecting the whole Christian world, Protestant
and Catholic alike.

A *Politisierung* of the Church would mean nothing
less than the death of evangelicism: it would open
a highway to Rome; it would mean the end of
the Reformation. The German struggle is only a
part of a decisive and world-wide battle going on
between the original theology of the Reformation
and the modern Protestantism of the last century,
between Christianity and Idealism. The revolution
of the "German Christians" is rendering the Evangelical Church signal service, since it reveals the
hidden abyss between these two forms of Protestantism. "An honest peace is achieved only by an
honest struggle"—not by decrees. That which
divides the two conflicting hosts is neither politics
nor power. The difference can most fittingly be
expressed in the historic words of Luther: "Yours
is a different spirit from ours!"

In this struggle between secularism and evangelical faith Karl Barth has uttered the prophetic
word: "The freedom of the Gospel may be repudiated by men in the Church, may be trodden
under foot. The Church may become desolate for
centuries. But the Gospel itself remains free, so
surely as God Himself remains free! And though
the Church be desolated, the true Church of God
lives invisibly in those who 'have not bowed the
knee to Baal,' but simply and joyfully confess the
name of the Lord."

(b) The Struggle for the Liberty of the Church

It is not only a struggle for purity of doctrine which has preoccupied those evangelical Christians in Germany who refused to accept the situation as it was. Perhaps even greater numbers within the Church have been involved in a struggle for the liberty of the Church. When the totalitarian State began to compel public institutions of all kinds to "tune in" (*gleichschalten*), it was soon clear that the Church could not hope to escape the application of the principle of unification and assimilation. How should the Church, having accepted the prince as *summus episcopus*, and having been from the days of the Reformation under State control, resist the general tendency in public life leading to unification of the whole people? Only a minority dared oppose the tendency.

This minority formed a party, *Church and Gospel*, which fought for the independence of the Church and claimed full liberty for administering it on the basis of its own evangelical principles. The nomination of Dr. F. von Bodelschwingh as head of the new Church of the Reich became a symbol of the struggle of the Church for evangelical liberty. Von Bodelschwingh, as we have stated before, did not receive sufficient backing by Church leaders, especially by the genuine Lutherans. His resignation left the field open to the growing aggressiveness of the "German Christians," who unblushingly claimed the right to have a majority in the synod and national assembly, to occupy most of the important posts in the Church, and to nominate for Reichsbishop a man of their own party, Ludwig Müller. The "Church and Gospel" group in the Prussian Synod struggled vainly against the policy and methods of the "German Christians," who were trying to apply the principles of Hitlerism to the Church and so bring it under State control. Finally, in protest, they withdrew from the synod, and twenty-two of their members, representing 3,000 pastors, drew up a declaration expressing deep concern over the loss of evangelical liberty in the Church and over the methods being used. But neither the exodus of the evangelical group nor their protest had any effect on the synod. The Church came under control of a group which advocated the closest relationship of State and Church, hailed Adolf Hitler as God-given leader, and approved the application of his anti-Semitic measures to ministers of the Church and professors in theological faculties as well as to public secular officials. The struggle for evangelical liberty has now become an open revolt. The "Church and Gospel" group complains that the methods employed have not been in conformity with Hitler's promise to respect the liberty of the Church, and that the ruling ecclesiastical party has interpreted that promise in its own interest. The conflict between the principle of a free Church and that of a national Church is most acute. It can only be settled ultimately, not by party decision, but by deeper theological reflection on the nature of the Church—reflection that "knows not the voice of a stranger," but only the voice of Christ.[1]

(c) The Struggle Against Racial Exclusiveness in the Church

It is a matter of gratification that of late opposition to anti-Semitism has been developing within the Church. Ever since the growing anti-Semitism led to boycotting of the Jews and to undeniable acts of violence and injustice, the Evangelical Churches in other European countries have been expecting a strong protest to come from the German Evangelical Church. But before the application of the Aryan paragraph to the Church came into effect, very few voices were raised against anti-Semitic outbreaks. Superintendent Dibelius of Berlin denounced these injustices, and the Conference of Roman Catholic bishops expressed its regret over certain acts of violence committed against the

[1] "It is seldom that politics and theology have ever been so closely interwoven as in this controversy. The confessional problem has assumed a political significance and the State has become an object of theological thought. . . . The present political crisis is interpreted as a religious crisis and the relationship between Church and world has become a dialectical problem. The Barthian 'dialectical' attitude was acknowledged as useful in the beginning of this crisis, but is now considered by a new national theology of creation and history to be '*ethisch unfruchtbar*,' since it is deemed unfit to give the practical solutions for the burning questions of contemporary life. A new way is opening for these advocates of a new theology : . . . faith in a leader leads to obedience and confidence in God . . . the religious revival of patriotism to faith in God and worship of His majesty. . . . National Socialism is thus becoming a confession in itself, tolerating no other *Weltanschauungs-Konfessionen* whatsoever." Hans Michael Müller, *Der innere Weg der deutschen Kirche*, Tübingen, 1933.

(These statements are the more important since Müller was the theological adviser of the Reichsbishop.)

Jews. Foreign protests were rebuffed by German Church leaders, as evidencing inadequate understanding of the situation and ignoring the main aspect of the German revolution, namely, the fight against atheistic and communistic Bolshevism. In comparison with this issue, the Jewish problem was declared to be a matter of minor importance. The right of the Government to readjust the proportion of Jews in public office was not questioned, although the methods used in carrying out this measure were deplored.

But from the time that the Aryan paragraph was put into effect in relation to the Churches, whereby a number of evangelical ministers and theologians were compelled to give up their posts, opposition to it within the Churches has been growing. This opposition has found voice in the declarations of various groups, especially in theological faculties. The theological faculty of Marburg,[1] for instance, in reply to a request from the Church in Hessen for a statement of opinion, issued a strong protest against the Aryan paragraph, the application of which was declared to be irreconcilable with the nature of the Evangelical Church which, according to the interpretation of the Reformation, is based on the sole authority of the Bible and the Gospel of Jesus Christ.

A similar statement was issued by a group of seventy professors of New Testament history, representing nearly all the German theological faculties. Their protest was sent to the National Synod and

[1] See Appendix IV.

was widely circulated. It was signed by the foremost scholars of the New Testament; by men like Bultmann in Marburg, Deissmann in Berlin, Heim in Tübingen, Jeremias in Greifswald, Jülicher in Marburg, Lietzmann in Berlin, Lueken in Frankfort, Lütgert in Berlin, Karl Ludwig Schmidt in Bonn, Schmitz in Münster, von Soden in Marburg, Windisch in Kiel, and many others. They stated, on September 23, 1933, "that the Christian Church, according to the New Testament, is composed of Jews and Gentiles who acknowledge Christ in the congregation; that membership in a Christian parish depends solely on faith and baptism; that, according to the New Testament, Jews and Gentiles alike were admitted to the ministry; that the Church has its origin in a call of God and the Holy Spirit, which makes no discrimination in the Church between members of various peoples or races; and that the Christian Church should stand for these principles in its doctrine and actions."[1]

The theological faculty in Erlangen supported this declaration as a general principle, but stated that "the sonship under God common to all Christians does not do away with the existing biological and social differences between men, but binds all to the class (*Stand*) in which they are called (by God). As it is our unescapable destiny to be bound together, from a biological standpoint, with a given group, Christians must recognize this fact in their thoughts and actions. To be one in Christ is, for the Lutheran confession of faith, not a matter of exterior organiza-

---

[1] Heim and a few others later withdrew their signatures.

tion, but of faith. The exterior order of the Church, according to the doctrine of the Reformation, must correspond not only to the universalism of the Gospel, but also to the historical and ethnographical structure (*Gliederung*) of the Christian people." The faculty sees this principle applied also in the building up of national or racial native Churches in the mission field. "The Church as such cannot decide whether the Jews in Germany really belong to the German people or whether they are an alien element (*Gastvolk*). Even baptism does not settle the question of whether, for instance, intermarriage between Jews and Christians is desirable or not. The whole question of the relation between Jews and Germans is a biological-historical problem and must be dealt with from this point of view. The Church must, therefore, recognize the right of the State to settle this problem by legal measures. The Church must support the principle of racial unity of the nation, and must, therefore, demand that Hebrew Christians refrain from exercising official functions in the Church. Their full membership in the German Evangelical Church is not contested, any more than that of other Christians who do not have the necessary qualifications for admission to office in the Church. This attitude, however, is not a rigid law, but allows exceptions from the general rule. Ministers of Jewish extraction who have already held office in the Christian Church should have the benefit of such exceptions. The right to make such exceptions in individual cases should be reserved for the bishops."

This statement, signed in the name of the faculty by Professors Althaus and Elert, is typical of the Lutheran attitude towards the State and the "law of nature," and represents a remarkable difference between the Lutheran and the Reformed conception of the relation between the Church and the world. The Reformed groups are generally less inclined to adopt for the Church principles and laws which belong to the natural order of the world. The Reformed Church of Frankfurt, for instance, and other Reformed bodies in the Rhineland, feel greatly concerned over the application of a biological principle to the Christian Church. The former refrained from voting in the Church assembly, leaving to the "German Christians" "full and sole responsibility for the shaping and administration of the Church."

Almost simultaneously the international bodies of the various œcumenical movements, in a spirit of fraternal discussion and with the strong desire to maintain the œcumenical relationship, expressed their grave concern over the attitude of the German Church towards Jewish Christians. After informal steps, taken by Church leaders in various countries, the committee of the *European Central Bureau for Inter-Church Aid*, assembled at Copenhagen, addressed an official letter to the German Church with a question as to what the German Church planned to do for the innocent victims of the Aryan paragraph, and whether co-operation with Churches abroad was desired. A committee of the *Œcumenical Council*, assembled at Novi Sad, and one representing the *World Alliance for Promoting International Friendship through the Churches*, realizing that the Evangelical Church was confronted with a mortal struggle for liberty and for purity of the Gospel which affected deeply the whole of Continental Protestantism and all œcumenical movements, expressed their concern over the situation in ways that did not impair friendly relations.

This pressure from abroad became stronger after the famous meeting at the Sportspalast in Berlin in January 1934, which proved a turning-point in the general judgment on the evangelical character of the "German Christian Movement," the Bishop of Chichester as president of the Universal Council on Life and Work, the Swiss Church Federation, the Scottish Churches and the Archbishop of Sweden expressed their disapproval of the application of the Aryan paragraph to the Church; and the American Federal Council of the Churches of Christ sent a personal representative to Berlin to protest not only against measures of violence and the abandoning of the legal basis of the Constitution, but also against the exclusiveness of a Christian Church based on racial considerations. Bishop Müller, in answer to this step, promised not only to withdraw the disciplinary measures, except those of a political character, but recognized a certain responsibility of the German Church for the fate of Christians of Jewish extraction.

Even the Aryan paragraph has become a theological problem treated by Professor Kittel and others in special publications.

VI

THE CHURCH IN A CHANGING WORLD

IN the former chapters we have stressed the spiritual forces and underlying theological ideas in the present religious situation on the Continent. We must now deal with the practical consequences. The questions arise: How does this revolution in ideas affect Church life? What are the effects of the present battle between new and old ideas on the structure of the Church, on its relation with the State, on its attitude towards its own educational and social activities, on inter-Church relations, and on the spiritual life of the congregations? We shall not confine this study to the German situation alone, although one can observe there more clearly than anywhere else the acute battle between the new and the old religious views.

I. THE STRUCTURE OF THE NEW CHURCH IN GERMANY

The leading aims in the reconstruction of the German Evangelical Church have been: (1) the preservation of the spiritual heritage of the Reformation; (2) the unification of the twenty-eight territorial Churches, hitherto associated in a loose federation, in one German Evangelical Church in which the Lutherans, by virtue of their numerical proportion, shall have a preponderant place, while at the same time the confessional rights of the Reformed minority are safeguarded; (3) the transformation of the consistorial and synodical constitution into an episcopal organization (at least so far as the Lutheran element is concerned); and (4) the establishment of a new relation to the National Socialist State upon the basis of mutual recognition and co-operation.

The German Evangelical Church declares that it stands on the unalterable foundation of the Gospel of Jesus Christ as witnessed in the Bible and interpreted afresh in the creeds of the Reformation. These basic principles determine and limit the power and authority of the Church in the fulfilment of its task.

The various provincial and territorial Churches united in the German Evangelical Church maintain their denominational independence and the traditional character of their worship, but the national Church has the right to unify the administration of these Churches by law. Other Church bodies of similar denominational character may become affiliated. The Constitution[1] has a unifying force in the relation of the Church to the State, of the new national Church to foreign religious bodies, and in the inter-relations of the educational, social and missionary activities within the Church.

A Lutheran Reichsbishop is entrusted with the

[1] See Appendix I.

leadership of the Church, and he represents it officially. He is supported in his task by an ecclesiastical ministry which includes three representative theologians and a legal adviser. A National Synod co-operates with him in the appointment of these ecclesiastical officials and in initiating Church legislation. Affiliated advisory commissions represent those free forces of the Christian people which hitherto have been organized in independent bodies for home and foreign missions, religious education and social service activity.

The Reichsbishop is endowed with unusual power: he represents the German Evangelical Church, he appoints its officials, and he has the right to publish official declarations in the name of the Church as a whole. He is nominated to the National Synod by the leaders of the Church and is elected by that Synod.

The ecclesiastical ministry, under his leadership, has the right not only to promulgate the laws of the Church voted by the National Synod, but also to legislate on its own authority. As stated above, its members are appointed by the Reichsbishop, on the recommendation of the Church leaders. The member representing the Reformed bodies acts for the Reichsbishop in all matters concerning that group.

The National Synod is composed of sixty members. Two-thirds of them are elected by the provincial Churches and one-third is freely appointed by the "ministers" of the National Church, on the basis of distinguished service in the Church.

The budget of the Church is raised by Church taxes in the provincial Churches.

It has been pointed out that, in spite of the close relation between Church and State, the new Church is not a "State" Church. Moreover, though the Church has become one administrative body, it is not a confessional union or fusion of the existing denominational bodies. Professor Sasse of Erlangen, however, considers the legal and administrative union a real Church union and sees in it the *coup de grâce* for the Lutheran Church. Several Lutheran bishops have protested against the preponderance given to representatives of the former United Church of Prussia.

In the increasing struggle between the Reichs-bishop and the bishops and their revolting pastors, Bishop Müller published a peace manifesto. But it was not accepted by large groups. The desire to transform the structure of the Church, especially the efforts to melt together the provincial independent Churches into one great national Church, met with vehement opposition, not only from pastoral groups led by men like Jacobi and Niemöller, and by Church leaders like Bishop Koch in Westfalen, Wurm in Württemberg, and Meiser in Bavaria, but in a growing measure also from congregations separating from the national Church and from "free Synods of witness," as in the Rhineland, Westfalen and in Southern Germany; these bodies show a marked tendency towards the formation of a free National Synod and the building up of an independent Evangelical Free Church.

2. CHURCH AND STATE

The various political and social revolutions in Europe have not only changed the face of the Continent and revolutionized the ideals of a whole generation, but have also deeply affected the relation between State and Church.

The Bolshevist State, or at least the ruling party in Russia, regarding religion as an opiate for the people, takes a definitely hostile attitude towards the Church, and sees in it a reactionary force, the influence of which must be shaken off by a new, secular, irreligious, anti-Christian type of education.

The neighbouring Polish State has Roman Catholicism for its State religion and tolerates other Churches without having given them as yet a legal status. Non-Catholic Churches in various parts of Poland are, therefore, still under the ecclesiastical laws of the States to which they belonged before the war: Protestant Churches in Posen under German Church law; in Galicia under the Austrian. The Orthodox Russian Church of Poland is under the former Russian Church law.

A new Church law to be promulgated is meant to deliver the Evangelical Churches entirely into the hands of the State.

A similar menace is hanging over the relations between the new Austrian State and the Evangelical Church. The State, having concluded a concordat with the Roman Church, is simultaneously trying to restrict the liberty of the Evangelical Church by special decrees which,

however, have resulted in a strong wave of reaction
—the conversion of thousands to the Evangelical
faith.

The Italian State, under Mussolini, has finally
realized the old ideal of Cavour, the Italian Bis-
marck, who desired a "free Church in a free State."
While granting a favoured position to the Roman
Church, the Government has, nevertheless, avoided
giving other confessions the appearance of being
merely "tolerated" Churches. It "admits" them
officially as long as they acknowledge the claims
of the State.

Since the separation of State and Church, in
1905, France has ignored the Churches except when
legal questions have been involved. It compels them
to form free religious associations and to apply for
State recognition before they can hold property.
The French Protestants early complied with these
demands and thereby entered into an official legal
relation with the State.

In the Spanish Revolution, after centuries of persecution and oppression, the State granted religious
liberty to the small Protestant minority.

Some States in central and eastern Europe maintain an official relation to the Lutheran or Reformed
or Orthodox Churches, but exclude other Protestant
bodies from legal recognition. Such is the case in
Austria and some of the States formerly belonging
to the Habsburg monarchy. Some of these Churches
even pay a small contribution called the *Congrua*
towards the budget of the established or State
Church.

In the Balkan countries the Orthodox Churches have always lived in closest relation with the nation and have maintained or awakened the national spirit in the oppressed people.

Most of the modern States, such as Holland, Switzerland and the Scandinavian countries, observe a friendly neutrality towards Church life, and cultivate a legally defined relation with the national Churches. In Sweden the Church even has the right of *veto* in all legal questions relating to its own interests.

The relation between State and Church in Germany has undergone considerable change since Hitler came into power. The Republic maintained an official relation to the Church, as established by law, and even paid the larger part of the salaries of the ministers and the budget of the theological faculties through its official channels, but it was, as a matter of fact, indifferent or hostile to the moral and religious functions of the Church. This was especially the case in certain of the local state units, such as Thuringia and Brunswick.

The new State of Adolf Hitler claims to be friendly to the Church, and seeks its collaboration in the effort to unify the nation and build up a new political and social organization. As the State seeks the Church, even so the Church seeks the State, recognizing its ideals and authority, and entering into so close a relation with this totalitarian State that it seems to many Free Churches abroad as if it had entirely surrendered its independence.

This situation has developed historically from

Luther's conception of the State and from the Lutheran theological conception of the relation between State and Church.

Luther was not a political thinker. He had, of course, no modern conception of the nature and function of the State. To his conservative thinking, the State was divinely ordered. It was represented authoritatively in the person of the prince, in accordance with Romans xiii. 1. The Government *was* the State. Even a bad Government had to be recognized as a provisional order which God had established in His wrath, or in His providence, to restrain the evil-doer, prevent chaos, and control the devil.

The State, according to this theory, is not based on the voluntary collective will of its members, not on any *contrat social*, as Rousseau said, but has its rational, ethical, and religious foundation in a direct act of God Himself, being an instrument of His providential care for men. The Government fulfils the Divine function of authority among men. It must, therefore, be obeyed in all secular affairs and accepted with a faith in God's inscrutable wisdom which tolerates even a bad ruler. A bad ruler is preferable to the destructive, chaotic, demoniac forces which rule the world of nature; and, at the right moment, God can always send a hero to deliver a people from a bad Government. One understands from this point of view why Luther is so popular in the State of Adolf Hitler. The great reformer has invested the ruler with so much religious authority that he can really claim to be fulfilling a Divine mission among his people—as millions of Christians in Germany actually believe he does. The German Church has always been accustomed to live in close relation with the State, and has seen no difficulty in recognizing the prince as supreme bishop, *summus episcopus*, of the territorial Church. It must be remembered in this connection that without the powerful protection of the God-fearing princes in the century of the Reformation the Evangelical Church could hardly have resisted the formidable hostility of the Emperor, who had put its reformer and founder under the ban.

It is easy to understand why contemporary German theology, trying to find an ethical and religious basis for the State, has fallen back on the theory of Luther. The theological literature of the last two years abounds in treatises and books dealing with the nature of the State and its relation to the Church.

Gogarten, for instance, a Lutheran professor and a friend of Karl Barth, has published a "political theology" based entirely on the principles of authority as established by Luther. The function of the State, as ordered by God, is to rule over the body and soul of its members. Only by using its authority and power in the midst of an evil world can the State prevent disintegration and chaos. Its authority contravenes the godless autonomy of the individual conscience characteristic of modern liberalism. For democracy there is no longer a place in the National Socialist State of Germany.

In a similar way another theological writer of

the Hitler State, William Stapel, in his book, *The Christian Statesman*, unites politics and theology as closely as possible. "Christ and Caesar belong together." An inner *nomos*, he says, an immanent law, is inherent in the blood of the nation, compelling it to develop all its God-given faculties to their highest possible degree. A superior nation is, therefore, called to occupy a dominant position in the hierarchy of nations and is under the God-given obligation to establish the *Reich*, that old mythical Empire, which had come to an end prematurely, under the levelling influences of modern democracy and liberalism. Neither the *Reich* nor the "nation" are to be understood merely as political postulates. They represent a religious eschatological ideal, which has the same mythical character as the idea of the "leader" (*der Führer*) who, far from being a usurper or a tyrant, is the mythical incarnation of the best qualities of the nation and hence is called to leadership and power. The Christian statesman must pave the way for the *imperium* of the best nation which, in turn, is to prepare for the coming Kingdom of Christ.

The old Lutheran concept of the State comes to light here. The State is not a democratic society, based on the equality of its members and ruled by an administration which is responsible to man-made laws, but is the *Obrigkeitsstaat*, represented by the ruler or the leader invested with Divine right, according to Romans xiii. 1, and responsible in his conscience to God alone. This conception of the State is widely glorified in Lutheran circles because, according to it, the State seems to be an institution more really responsible to God, the Supreme Ruler, than it is in the legalistic, Calvinistic and Western conception of the State, in which the latter is merely a society with a succession of magistrates, cabinets and parliaments, without any direct and personal responsibility towards a supreme Divine Power. The Government in a Calvinistic State has no authority other than that of changeable laws and articles. The German people are not simply indulging in hero-worship: they have clad their leader in the religious glory of a Messiah sent by God Himself to deliver His people from dishonour, slavery and misery. They hail him as their mystically appointed *Führer* even though he rules them with a rod of iron. The new National Socialist State in Germany, therefore, is founded not only on the hero-worship of an enthusiastic nation or on the political will of a party, but on a well-elaborated system of metaphysics and an underlying theology of the State.

Nevertheless, the new unified Church rejects—in theory, at least—the application of political principles to the constitution of the Church. "The German Evangelical Church is no State-established Church," declares Reichsbishop Müller, in an official statement sent to the Churches abroad. Not political convictions, but the Gospel of Jesus Christ, as witnessed by the Bible and by the confessions of faith of the reformers, are basic for the German Evangelical Church. The Church has, indeed, given up its former indifferent neutrality towards the State—but such neutrality is not based on evangelical doctrine. The Church feels a new responsibility for the State in which it has to live, whose protection it enjoys: she feels bound to co-operate with it in a common service for the moral and social welfare of the people.

"The State cannot be ruler of the Church," declares Reichsbishop Müller, "but it is none the less a gift of God which we must recognize." It is a matter of gratification for the Church to see that "the new German State similarly acknowledges the activity of the Church, with a will to further it and to give it the place in the community of the nation and the liberty which it needs for the fulfilling of its task."

The State rebukes any so-called liberal freedom of conscience which would lead arbitrarily towards the disintegration of all order. But it recognizes the spiritual liberty of conscience claimed by the reformers, and furthers it. "The State remains State and the Church remains Church." The Reichsbishop demands mutual confidence, therefore, as the fundamental basis of the relation between State and Church.

We have shown in our last chapter that there are large groups which have no confidence in the new Government and in the ruling party of the Church. These groups, represented by individuals like Karl Barth, by the "Young Reformation Movement," and by a number of other organizations, cannot easily forget the spirit and the methods by which the ruling party came into power. They cannot reconcile themselves to the repressive measures which the Reichsbishop has seen fit to use increasingly. Nor can they acknowledge that the underlying theology of the situation is truly evangelical. They deplore the lack of clear theological thinking. As we have seen in the last chapter, they are afraid lest, in a relationship so close, the Church may become an instrument in the hands of the State, the Gospel may become adulterated, and the spiritual life of the Church be crippled.

3. THE CHURCH AND THE PEOPLE

Following the Reformation, national Churches were established in all evangelical countries, according to the principle, *cujus regio ejus religio*, which is to say, that the ruler of the State had the right to determine which religion should be imposed on his people. These national or provincial Churches presupposed the existence of a Christian State composed of the whole Church and the whole people. This conception of the Church, as being composed of all Christian people of the same faith living in one country, has prevailed in recent times only in certain northern countries, such as Sweden —where it was against the law to leave the Church —and Finland—where nearly 98 per cent of the people are still members of the national Lutheran Church. The rise of "free" Churches, together with the religious indifference of modern times, has dissolved the mediaeval idea of the identity between the Christian people in any State and the State Church. Large masses have lost all contact with

149

the Church. This is true of both cultured and labouring classes—the two extremes of society. Modern civilization has drifted more and more towards a religion of science, without creed and without cult. The working classes—or, at least, their leaders—have found in Marxism a new religion, with its own prophets, its own faith in a new and better fellowship among men, its own eschatology and its own symbols. Having lost contact with these groups, the Church has found its stronghold in the lower middle class.

In France, for instance, out of forty million people the Roman Catholic Church claims barely ten millions; the Protestant Churches not quite one million. The remaining twenty-eight or twenty-nine millions are an easy prey to modern indifference, scepticism or agnosticism. They constitute a huge mission field for the Christian Churches. Where Marxism, capitalism and communism have become predominant influences in western, central and northern Europe, a shallow materialism and a religion of "this worldliness" has threatened the spiritual life of the national Churches.

The Churches have reacted strongly against this wave of modern paganism. The Free Churches of various denominational origins, such as the Moravians, Methodists, Baptists, the Gospel Christians and the Salvation Army, are working as missionary bodies among the indifferent masses, and the national Churches themselves have formed special organizations for home missions and evangelization. The Evangelical Society in France has become a real Church builder, and the "Inner Mission" in Germany and Austria has built up a huge organization for charitable work. The *Rauhes Haus*, in Hamburg, founded by Wichern, the settlement of Bethel, near Bielefeld, under Pastor von Bodelschwingh, the deaconess-house at Kaiserwerth, the religious educational centres, the work of evangelization and the Christian Press may be cited as examples of the activities of these bodies.

Besides these evangelical forces within the Church, there is the Christian Workmen's Union. This has developed in Germany, Holland and Switzerland, and now has millions of members. The Workers' Movement thus has to-day three world-centres: a Communist Internationale in Moscow, a Socialist (and strongly Marxian) centre in Amsterdam, and the Christian centre in Utrecht, Holland. The two latter movements have received a severe blow from the Fascist and National Socialist revolutions in Italy and Germany, where the workers' unions have been merged with the national workers' organization of the Government.

The new Church in Germany is fully aware of the tremendous educational task with which it is confronted in the present situation. "The struggle for the soul of a people has begun," Reichsbishop has declared. The "people's mission," taking up the former home mission work, will endeavour to awaken new spiritual life in the masses which, under pressure from the official nationalistic religions, are flowing back to the Church. Evangelical academies have already been founded to train missionary leaders in the knowledge of the religious and national ideals of the new Church.

It is one of the principles of the Church in Germany to transform the former "pastors' Church" into a "people's Church," and to win back for the Church the cultured people as well as the labour folk, who had largely left it. But here again a theological consideration comes in, the question, namely, whether a "people's Church"—including everybody as members—is really a truly Evangelical Church, or whether it must be built exclusively on free members confessing the historical faith of the Church. Theologians like Barth and Weinel would be afraid of shutting up the masses in a Reformed or other confessional "ghetto." The Church for them is not a society of saints, but that acre of the Bible which includes both wheat and tares.

4. THE CHURCH AND THE WORLD

The Church turns its face not only towards Heaven and God's Eternal Word, but towards the finite world where lie its concrete tasks, and where she enters into fraternal fellowship with the Christians of various countries and Churches. The attitude of the Church towards the world is the determining factor in judging the present Church political struggle. Whilst Karl Barth, for instance, fixes his eyes almost exclusively on the Divine message of the Church and elaborates an absolutist theology which is concerned with nothing but the Word of God and pure doctrine, other theologies, without denying this Divine impulse, are more concerned with the realization of the Word in the practical work of the Church—the progressive incarnation of the eternal *logos* in the flesh and blood of humanity.

(a) *What is the World?*

Wherever the Church speaks of the revelation of God, she also speaks *of* and *to* the world. Her conception of God involves a definite conception of the world itself. Every theology includes an "anthropology," and German theologians like Gogarten and Bultmann propose to make anthropology the starting-point for theological thinking.

In a time of prosperity, conquest, and courageous enterprise, it is easy to attribute an optimistic significance to the meaning of the world. It becomes the place of God's good creation, the plastic element for man's good will.

The World War and its aftermath have profoundly altered this optimistic conception. Man, confronted with the world as it is to-day, cannot help judging it pessimistically. He is deeply moved by a "tragic sense of life" as Unamuno, the Spanish philosopher, expresses it. The optimistic happiness of the orderly life of the Victorian era and of prosperous capitalism has passed. The pessimistic interpretation of the world as given in the Bible again comes to the front.

The world is a fallen creation, the place where God's message meets opposition and hostility, where Christians must fight against "principalities and powers," against "spiritual wickedness in high places."

The world is doomed. God's judgment is hanging over it—but also God's grace. This eschatological conception of the world has largely influenced not only Lutheran and Calvinistic theology, but also the attitude of the Churches—at least, in Germany —towards practical problems such as peace, and towards new tasks placed before her by the economic and industrial crisis of to-day.

(b) What Shall We Do?

This earnest question reflects the impulse towards social activity in the Church. The strongest of social impulses is Christian love. In the commandment of love, Christ gave lasting inspiration to live a life of full responsibility towards one's neighbour and of unreserved sympathy towards one's brethren.

But this commandment is not an elaborated social programme. The Christian conscience must always rediscover what Christian love means in terms of the immediate necessities of life and in concrete practical tasks. For a long time "Christian love" meant those practical works of Christian charity which left no poor Lazarus uncared for, no weak brother unprotected, no abandoned children forlorn. Such Protestant saints as Wichern in Germany, George Müller in Bristol, Father von Bodelschwingh in Bethel, Pastor Fliedner in Kaiserwerth, and John Bost in France, gave a new interpretation of what Christian love means in a world of distress and despair. They built up within the Christian Church that wonderful work of the "Inner Mission" which is fulfilling the Good Samaritan's task in western and central Europe. The Protestant and Orthodox Churches of eastern Europe are only just beginning to introduce this charitable activity among their people.

The new economic and industrial problems have compelled the Churches of Europe to find new, more efficient and more comprehensive interpretations of Christian love and fellowship. Charity must be supplemented by a new knowledge of facts and by a programme of social reform. Various Churches in Europe—in Great Britain, France, Germany and Switzerland—have already adopted such a programme. The "religious social movement" has sprung up (partly influenced by the American "Social Gospel") under the leadership of men like Kutter and Ragaz in Switzerland, Tillich and Fuchs in Germany, Elie Gounelle in France, Slotemaker in Holland and Manfred Bjoerquist in Sweden.

The attempts to interpret the Gospel as a healing and constructive force in the present economic and industrial chaos are focussed on an international Christian basis in the *International Christian Social Institute* at Geneva. This is the laboratory and agency of the Universal Christian Council for Life and Work, which grew out of the World Conference held at Stockholm in 1925. The Institute stimulates social welfare activities in the Churches through its research department, by arranging study conferences in various countries. These conferences deal, from a theological as well as from a sociological

155

point of view, with the questions of the new structure of society, unemployment and other pressing problems of our times.

It is a fact worthy of wide attention that the collaboration of the Churches in the field of these social problems leads back to the study of the ultimate underlying theological conceptions on which the various Churches originally based their activity—just as in the field of Church polity theology, by clarifying fundamental questions, is assigned the duty of preparing the way for the solution of the secondary problems of structure and practical activity.

The Churches do not all derive the practice of social service from the same underlying fundamental principles of theological ethics. The *Orthodox Church*, despite her traditional ritualism, mysticism, and sacramentalism, finding herself confronted to-day with the same social problems as in the Western world, sees in the commandment of Christian charity a sufficient principle for the application of the Gospel to the needs of our time.[1]

The *Lutherans*[2] admit that their fundamental confession of faith, the *Augustana*, gives no clear social doctrine. For those who hold to the Augsburg Confession, the social problem is, consequently, not

[1] So Professor Alivisatos, Athens, and Professor Zankow, Sofia, at a study conference in Bukarest, arranged by the Christian Social Institute, in Geneva.

[2] Schoeffel and Koeberle, *Luthertum und Sociale Frage*, Leipzig, 1931.

a Christian, but a secular one. Spiritual and temporal things must be clearly differentiated. For God created two orders: Church and State. "The social problem is primarily a concern not of the Church, but of the State. But the State also comes from God—is, indeed, one of the primary orders of God's creation." The present social disorder is a flagrant contradiction of God's created orders, and, therefore, an appeal must be made to all Christians, as well as to the State, to combat evil in society. But man has fallen into sin, and this tragic fact excludes all humanistic idealism of the type that glorifies human possibilities and dreams of working out all-embracing, redemptive social programmes. As sin is the real root of the prevailing social evils, the Church must begin its work with the assurance of grace, not with the idealistic hope "of transforming the world by its vigilance and effort into the Kingdom of God." This world is under the power of Satanic influences. It remains for God, at the Last Judgment, to conquer these powers. This conception may not seem to give unreserved inspiration to social activity; but in the midst of this hopeless world there is at work also the "Word of God." An outstanding Lutheran like Bishop Schoeffel interprets this Word as a stimulating and efficient "force from God, which leads us not to sweet inner experiences nor to mere doctrinal statements," but to "public activity and to practical decisions, which the concrete situation imperiously demands from the Church."

Emil Brunner has published an "Ethics,"[1] based on *Reformed principles* (though Karl Barth would not recognize it as genuinely Calvinistic). In this volume he declares that God has placed man in the midst of this world. The good is nothing else than His will. Good is what is ordered and inspired by God alone. Our right relationship towards the world, our social activity, must come first from this knowledge of God and from humble obedience to Him, not from ethical idealism; from the full acceptance of God's justification by faith, not from an axiomatic "social gospel," nor from a general moral principle of Christian ethics. Brunner is as strongly opposed to the legalist spirit pervading Reformed ethics as he is to the quietist tendency—which, incidentally, he does not find in Luther himself, but only in later Lutheran orthodoxy, the result of the influence of Melanchthon. A legalist interpretation of God's will, the conception of grace as an infused moral power, leads towards the rigid prohibitive ethics of Puritanism, an ethics derived much more from the *lex naturae* in man, from the conscience as such, from the general moral Christian ideal, from the philosophic conception of the highest values, than from the living Word of God. God's pardon and justification, rightly understood, do not lead to quietism, but to a reshaping of our life and our concrete relations to the brethren, in a spirit of faith and obedience. Only in this sense is the Church, as Karl Barth calls it, "a vanguard of God."

Brunner sees the real solution of the ethical

[1] *Das Gebot und die Ordnungen*, Tübingen, Mohr, 1932.

158

problem in a deeper rethinking of the ethical basis of our existence itself. His argument may be summarized as follows:

Only in so far as we have first listened to God's will in His word, inviting us to believe and to obey, are we able to answer the question: "What shall we do?" The first commandment of God is "Come and believe!" The acceptance of this call enables us to understand what our next step shall be—a step which we cannot know in advance through legalist prescription. "The law should not be identified with God's commandment; obedience of faith is different from submission to law." The law becomes God's commandment only when it is vivified by God's direct appeal. We do not know what the law really means, not even the law of love—until it is illuminated and interpreted to us by God's Spirit, which makes it present and concrete.

"We never can know by ourselves in advance what God's will is." Neither nature nor conscience reveals to us this mystery. Only God Himself can show us what is His will. He does so by placing Christ before us. In Christ He gives us His own life, enabling us to know His will and to do it. It is not for us to interpret the Divine law of love. He Himself does this, as His part in that act of faith which is the free acceptance of God's free gift.

Faith cannot be separated from action, else it would be a mere theory without the act of obedience. This, then, is the true basis of all Christian ethics:

159

It does not lie in rules or orders or values, but in the absolute readiness to obey God's commandment of love. This alone is absolute and permanent; this alone does not grant moral vacations, "for it is the real condition of life." To oppose it means ruin and death.

If, then, we ask what God's will is concretely, the revelation in the Bible gives the answer: God's will is hidden in this world with all its individual aspects, with its countless irrational riddles. We must have a certain reverence for a world which is God's creation—reverence before it on account of its Creator, and not, as Albert Schweitzer teaches in his *Philosophy of Culture*, reverence for life as such. In this concrete world we discover certain traces of God's will, a given hierarchy of values. The world is not the plastic element which is ours to form, as Idealism thinks. It contains certain immanent forms which we can only discover and respect. God's law does not, therefore, hover above the world as an abstract ethical idea. We meet it in this concrete world in the fatal moment when His call definitely challenges us.

But we must remember that this world wherein we live is a world of sin. God's will in this world is, therefore, veiled and distorted. God wills this world and negates it simultaneously. The will of God cannot be identified with the world as it is, but we must seek it in this given world with a view towards the world to come. To stand in the attitude of always being ready to accept God's claim upon us and the challenge of love which meets us in our brother, and to let ourselves be used as God's instruments, is fundamental for evangelical ethics.

The commandment of love is one, but its forms are many. There are no fixed rules for these forms; even the Sermon on the Mount gives no absolute rule. It is an "occasional" example which does not liberate us from the personal responsibility of finding the specific form of God's commandment in the given situation which confronts us. Every legalist interpretation of God's will must be avoided. Man is placed not before a "*code civil*," but is confronted with God Himself and His infinite claim upon us to which we can respond only in an ever renewed act of personal decision.

A Protestant ethics must defend its liberty of responsibility against the legalist conception of the Roman Catholic ethics, as well as against the well-known ethical attitudes of libertinism and quietism. The task of ethics is not to decide anything in advance, but to prepare for the personal decision of the Christian in a given moment and in a concrete situation.

This does not exclude our conforming to the orders found in nature, in our social surroundings, in law and in the Bible, but these orders, until we enter into a direct personal relationship with God Himself, have only a provisional and educational value in the world of sin. The motive of Christian ethics is not a general idea of the highest good, nor a written, exterior law, nor a supreme value which we have to realize, nor conscience, which is only the alarm signal of something wrong in man, "the flaming sword between God and man." It is simply this personal responsibility towards God, our Creator and Redeemer.

The practical application of this fundamental responsibility begins when an *I* is confronted with a *Thou*. The "neighbour," in his claim upon us, becomes the representative of God's claim upon us.

This general thesis, wh'ch issues from a new understanding and appreciation of the thought of Luther and Calvin, is then developed by Brunner with reference to the various social orders.

The typical *Anglican* or, at least, Anglo-Catholic theology derives its social ethics from the law of the Incarnation, which refers not only to the individual fact of the appearance of Christ, but to the progressive realization of the eternal *Logos* in flesh and blood in the substance of this world. At the same time, the idea of the Church and the symbolic interpretation of its liturgy inspires Anglicans with an ideal of fellowship and a sacramental sanctification of life which are highly stimulative to social work.

These underlying theological principles[1] have not failed to influence deeply the practical activity of the Churches. Lutheranism, looking upon the world as the domain of Satan, is inclined to leave social activities to the State or to individual Christian

[1] The various theological principles underlying the social activity of the Churches have been set forth in a comparative study, published by the Christian Social Institute at Geneva, under the title: *Kirche, Bekenntnis Sozial Ethos.* Geneva, 1934.

initiative. This world must suffer war, distress and all kinds of evil until God delivers it at the end by His judgment and His victory. Calvinism, on the other hand, has always been much concerned with knowing and doing the will of God in practical life. An "activist" conception of social ethics came into force in Calvinism which found its strongest exponent in Western Christianity.

(c) Foreign Missions

Continental Christianity is feeling the same crisis in foreign and home missionary work as the American Churches, but from another point of view. While mission work is one of the salient features in the life of American Protestantism, the Continental Churches have left missionary work largely to individual missionary societies. These societies have been in close connection with the Church and have been inspired by its message, but have built up foreign missions under their own responsibility. A blessed work has been done, not only by the great English and Scottish missionary societies and Church boards, but also by Continental missionary societies of Germany, Switzerland, France, Holland and the Scandinavian countries. The Churches in eastern Europe, more concerned with the struggle for their existence, have been able, for the most part, to take up missionary work only to a very small extent.

It is not our task here to give a survey of European missions. Suffice it to say that the large part of the Continental societies are not so much concerned with social work in the mission field, or with the expansion of distinct denominational Churches competing with each other, as with individual conversions and the founding of native, indigenous Churches. Humanist or syncretist tendencies are not affecting our missionary societies so much as is the economic crisis. Barthianism is also having its effect, for it has raised the fundamental question whether Churches have the right to be concerned on the mission field with educational and social aims, or whether they must not adhere strictly to their unique task of preaching the Gospel of Jesus Christ to a world of sinners. The old missionary motives are further complicated by the Barthian teaching that both Christians and pagans are sinners, in need of the pardon of God.

5. REVOLUTION AND SPIRITUAL LIFE

During and after the war the evangelical Churches on the Continent passed through years of incredible suffering. Hunger, distress and poverty, fear and despair have been frequent guests in many parishes, evangelical institutions, manses and evangelical homes in sixteen countries.

But this time of need has nevertheless been a period of great spiritual blessing. As often in the course of the history of the Christian Church, suffering, distress and persecution have proved to be a source from which new spiritual life has sprung forth. Faith has been tested in these tribulations. Need has stimulated the Christian energies to the